THE AUBURN UNIVERSITY ❧

WALKING

TOUR GUIDE

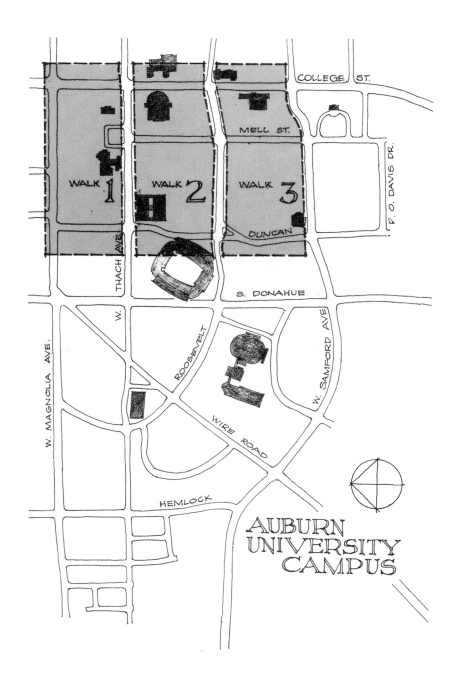

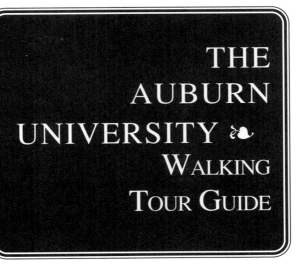

THE AUBURN UNIVERSITY ❧ WALKING TOUR GUIDE

R. G. Millman

The University of Alabama Press
TUSCALOOSA • LONDON

Book design by Bob Nance, Auburn class of 1957

Library of Congress Cataloging-in-Publication Data

Millman, R. G.
The Auburn University walking guide / R. G. Millman.
p.   cm.
Includes bibliographic references (p.) and index.
ISBN 0-8173-0523-8 (alk. paper)
1. Auburn University—Description. 2. Auburn University—Guide
books. 3. Auburn University—History. I. Title.
LD271.A6615M55   1990   90–44978
378.761'55—dc20

British Library Cataloguing-in-Publication Data available

Contents

Preface

A NUMBER OF PEOPLE WITH SPECIAL INTEREST IN Auburn, the town and the University, have preceded me in recording the facts, the stories, and the myths of this place. I thank them for their scholarship. From them I have borrowed heavily in putting together this guide and to them I owe much. Some are no longer with us, but their legacy of notes and documents remains. I am a newcomer to this community, having arrived a scant twenty-two years ago, but after completing this study, I feel a part of the evolving tradition that makes up Auburn.

Others have given much needed encouragement and positive feedback. First of all, I thank President James Martin and the University administration for supporting this project. Tony Hyder, especially, coached me in ways to approach the assignment. Members of the Draughon Library staff were very helpful and patient, especially those indulgent people who work in the archives and in special collections. I called on faculty members with intimate knowledge of particular buildings. Among them were Professors Cleveland Harrison and Nicholas Davis and Dean John T. Vaughan. The University Relations Office loaned me the services of Roy Summerford, who did a careful reading of the first draft and offered solid suggestions. The Office of the University Architect, through Orlando Moron, furnished a number of vital documents. The up-to-date information concerning the veterinary school was graciously supplied by Marion Moore.

I am indebted to Malcolm MacDonald, Director of The University of Alabama Press, for the initial suggestion that a campus guide might be a timely idea. Robert Mellown, whose guide to The University of Alabama was a model, made many insightful and invaluable comments on my first submittal. Joanne Patton sat patiently at the word processor through countless revisions and has earned my everlasting gratitude. The ultimate editor on issues of grammar, punctuation, and the sound of the prose was my wife, Mary, and I thank her sincerely.

R. G. M.
AUBURN UNIVERSITY

Other Sources

A great many documents have been combed, scanned, perused, and analyzed to extract the material that forms the substance of this guide. *Auburn, Loveliest Village of the Plains* is a personalized history of the town by Mollie Hollifield. Other sources include *Auburn, A Pictorial History of the Loveliest Village* (The Donning Company, 1981), put together with great good humor by Jack Simms and Mickey Logue, *Lengthening Shadows* (Auburn University, 1977), edited by L. B. Williams, and *Through the Years, Auburn from 1856* (Auburn University, 1977), an accounting of the administration of each of Auburn's presidents written by two professors of history, Malcolm McMillan and Allen Jones.

Sam Brewster, a longtime director of buildings and grounds, wrote a very useful *General History of Alabama Polytechnic Institute, 1856–1959*. It is an unpublished paper later revised by L. E. Funchess, his successor, and L. B. Williams.

The scholarship of two graduate students representing two quite different eras at Auburn was instructive. Roger S. Sparks wrote *A Handbook of The Alabama Polytechnic Institute* in 1935. It is a history of the institution's first sixty-nine years. Then, in 1988, Eliza-

beth D. Schafer wrote *Reveille for Professionalism—
Alabama Veterinary Medical Association, 1907–1952,*
which is, in part, a history of Auburn's School of Veterinary Medicine. Both are unpublished master's theses.

Other regular University publications provided a rich
source of information: the *AU Report,* the *Auburn
Alumnews,* news releases from the University Information Office, and the yearbook, *Glomerata.* The local
newspapers regularly carry stories about the campus
and its building program: the *Opelika-Auburn News* and
the *Auburn Bulletin.* Ann Pearson has written often for
both papers, and I have borrowed freely from her. Neil
Davis, former owner-publisher of the *Bulletin* and later
a professor of journalism at Auburn, wrote a number of
colorful accounts of life as it was lived in the loveliest
village in years past.

The Passing Parade

I came to Auburn in 1968 as a stranger to this community with which I have now become so familiar. My
perspective is certain to be somewhat different from
that of a native or a loyal alumnus. The passing parade
of students will have special feelings for the buildings
and spaces on campus that were memorable to them
during their tenure. In a frank discussion of the structures that constitute the campus, one runs the risk of not
giving equal time to all, or of revealing skeletons, or of
treading on some toes by not showing proper respect for
certain icons. But I hope that the picture of the campus
presented here is an honest and balanced one, and that
the reader will enjoy peeling back some of the layers
of time, history, and nostalgia that wrap these campus
facades.

Illustrations

THE PHOTOGRAPHS IN THIS BOOK ARE FROM A VARIETY OF sources. I thank them all for their participation in this project: the University Archives, the Office of University Relations, Photographic Services, and students from my Photo I course. Other photographs were taken by me. The illustrations also include renderings from the offices of the architects involved in particular building projects.

Interspersed with these are some of my own drawings and paintings, including the front cover, done over a period of years. They are some of my favorite subjects on campus and represent buildings with which I have had intimate and long-standing association. They are included to offer a change of pace from the black-and-white photos and because I enjoy doing them.

Campus Planning

MAJOR DEVELOPMENT OF THE AUBURN CAMPUS came after the period of frenetic expansion of new colleges and universities that swept the country from 1820 to the Civil War. There is no record of a grand scheme set down by the founders to create a Beaux Arts axial order for the future, as there was for many other fledgling campuses. Attempts to create a master plan came later, when a logical framework for development became an imperative generated by the accelerating rate of growth.

Several prominent, nationally recognized planning firms—including the Olmsted Brothers, Harland Bartholomew and Associates, and most recently, Johnson, Johnson, and Roy—have been commissioned through the years to study the campus situation and create a master plan. Each of these well-documented proposals has generated heated discussion and considerable resistance. All have failed in the end to gain total acceptance. The Department of Physical Plant has also taken its turn at shaping plans to direct campus growth and development. One of those plans is included in this guide.

The firm of the Olmsted Brothers grew out of a legacy left by their father, the celebrated Frederick Law Olmsted, who was responsible for the planning of at least twenty campuses in America, including Stanford University in California. He originated a prototypical

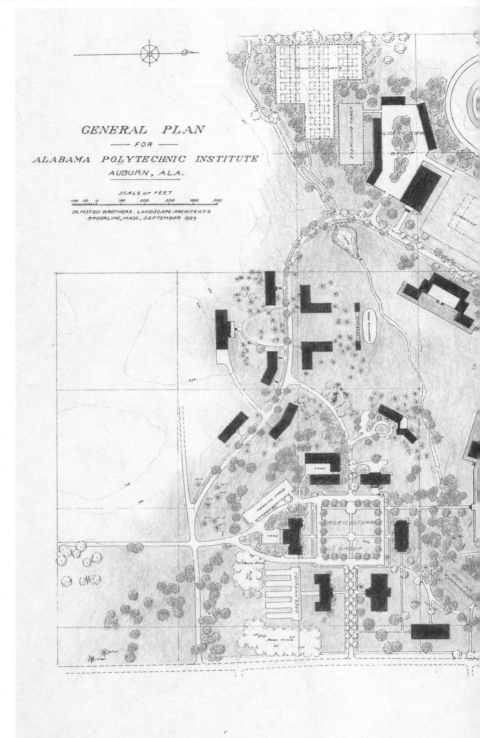

GENERAL PLAN
— FOR —
ALABAMA POLYTECHNIC INSTITUTE
AUBURN, ALA.

SCALE OF FEET

OLMSTED BROTHERS, LANDSCAPE ARCHITECTS
BROOKLINE, MASS., SEPTEMBER 1929

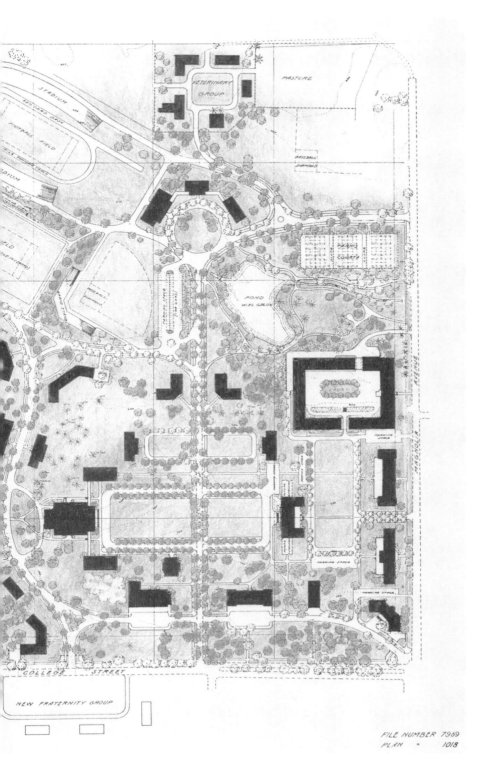

VETERINARY GROUP

PASTURE

BASEBALL DIAMOND

STADIUM

FOOTBALL FIELD

TENNIS COURTS

POND
W.E.L. GREEN

MAGNOLIA AVENUE

COLLEGE STREET

NEW FRATERNITY GROUP

FILE NUMBER 7969
PLAN " 1018

layout for land-grant schools based on "a democratic idealism and a commitment to the welfare of the working classes." His ideals led him to reject monumental massing in favor of informal arrangements of small structures placed in a semirural setting. His two sons carried on the work of the firm with a dedication to the same fundamental philosophy.

The Olmsted Brothers were working closely with President Bradford Knapp in 1928–29, just before the Great Depression put an abrupt end to many ambitious schemes. A copy of their plan is included here. It is dated September 1929, the month before the fateful October stock market crash that plunged the country into a devastating depression. The scheme is filled with optimism, providing generous dormitory groupings complete with swimming pool, an abundance of tennis courts, reflecting ponds, and a large complex of athletic facilities. It combines formal Renaissance planning with an informal meandering curvilinear street layout that is typical Olmsted. Whether the plan even received a formal review by the board of trustees is unknown. Its fate, along with that of some ambitious building plans being promoted by President Knapp, was sealed by the disastrous downturn in the economy.

In 1978, the Atlanta office of Harland Bartholomew and Associates undertook the task of shaping plans to guide growth of the University through 1995, by which time they projected an enrollment of 21,500 students. A major part of their comprehensive plan dealt with the traffic and parking problem. Recommendations included the erection of three parking decks and the placing of extensive student parking lots on the periphery. The firm also recommended that the central area of the campus become part of an academic core and that the residential uses of that area be relocated. Their report projected the inevitability of a shuttle bus system to move students and faculty between classes, offices, labs, and dorms.

The latest master planning effort was completed in 1988 by the firm of Johnson, Johnson, and Roy's Dallas office. At the time this guide was prepared, it had

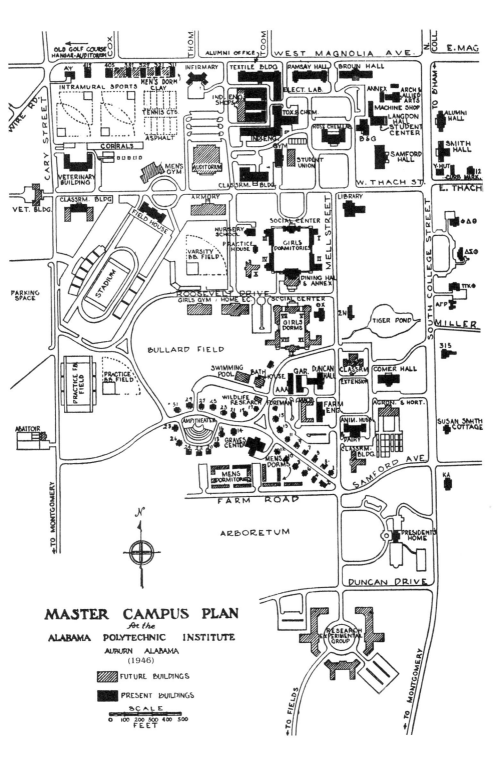

not been released for publication. But preliminary meetings with the planners indicate their recommendations are similar to the Bartholomew group: create an academic core, relegate the auto to the periphery, and turn the campus into a pedestrian mall with free bus rides provided when distances are great. It is a major change and difficult to envision, but it may be Auburn's future.

THE
AUBURN
UNIVERSITY &

WALKING
TOUR GUIDE

Introduction

AUBURN HAS ALWAYS BEEN "AUBURN." EVEN WHEN it was the East Alabama Male College (1856), the Agricultural and Mechanical College of Alabama (1872), Alabama Polytechnic Institute (1899), and finally Auburn University (1960), the institution has always been known as *Auburn*, shedding the mantle of those earlier pretentious institutional labels in favor of a friendlier tone.

A brief history of the beginnings of Auburn University seems a proper introduction to this guide to campus buildings. Auburn is a colorful and spirited place, as the story of individual buildings recorded here will illustrate. In collecting background material, I have relied heavily on the writings of others, including an unofficial historian and chronicler, Ann Pearson, through her regular column in the *Opelika-Auburn News*. The quotations below are taken from one of her accounts.

Auburn was destined to be a center for education. The town's founder, Judge John Harper, had dreams of creating a religious and educational center when he led a small settlement party from Harris County, Georgia, to the site in 1836. One of Judge Harper's first acts was to donate a plot of land for a Methodist church, and the log cabin erected thereon doubled as a one-room school. Later, across the street, land for the first public school was dedicated. The first college-level institution in the town was established for the education of genteel young ladies. Its charter, granted by the Masonic Lodge in 1852, included a prohibition on the sale of strong spirits within a two-mile radius of the campus. The school was situated in the town's center where the Auburn National Bank now stands. It was quite successful.

With 400 young lady pupils in the town of only 1,000 inhabitants in the 1850s the focal point of Auburn was already becoming its education institution, though the prosperity that enabled families to send their female off-spring to learn wax work came from a cotton-slave economy.

Wax work was not the only subject taught, of course. Ancient languages, piano and vocal lessons, guitar playing, and the science of chemistry were also part of the curriculum. For an extra twelve dollars per term, a student could also take needlepoint or modern language. The basic tuition for the five month term was twenty dollars. Room and board added another fifty dollars—figures that are hard to believe today.

Efforts by the Methodists to start a college for males were supported by the entire town. Citizens raised an impressive $100,000 earnest money in the early 1850s, and the East Alabama Male College was chartered in 1856 after heated debate in the Alabama legislature and over Governor John Anthony Winston's veto.

One of its chief enticements, besides the presence of genteel young ladies and the railroad, was the absence of spiritous liquors. . . .

The college did not open until 1859 in a large, graystone, four-story building, called Old Main (or The Main), built for $111,000. This college forswore wax work for the classical, liberal arts education, and its activities soon merged with the educational program of the Female College. Professors such as Darby taught combined classes of young men and women, and the chapel was used for many Male College events.

The Male College had a faculty of six, a college enrollment of 80, and preparatory enrollment of 100, making it considerably smaller than the female institution

The Rev. William J. Sasnett was the first president, and five students graduated that first year. By 1860, enrollment rose to 101 students and the preparatory enrollment to 127.

The Civil War closed both institutions, though records do not show exactly when the Female College closed. The Male College closed in 1861. Langdon Hall today holds a wall plaque honoring the students who served in the Confederate forces.

The Female College never reopened after the War. One of the few reminders of it today is a boulder with an embedded plaque, placed early in this century by the U.D.C., that lies on the north side of Auburn National Bank.

The East Alabama Male College, though badly crippled, did reopen its doors in 1866, after the War. Although the facilities were in place, the Methodist church did not have the money to fund the college adequately. Relief came in the form of federal legislation, the Morrill Act of 1862, which provided public lands and maintenance money to support a college in each state "where the object shall be . . . to teach such branches of learning as are related to agriculture and the mechanical arts in order to promote the liberal and practical education of the industrial classes in the several pursuits and professions in life."

The Methodists offered the complete college facilities plus two hundred acres to the state. In 1872, the state accepted the bid and the Agricultural and Mechanical College of Alabama came into being.

The change signaled a shift in emphasis, from a concentration on classic Greek and Latin education to more scientific and pragmatic concerns. As noted in *Through the Years*, "To the new faculty of eight, four from the former liberal arts college and four new professors, fell the task of developing the knowledge and techniques of instruction to accomplish the intent of the Morrill Act."

There were inevitable conflicts between the traditional and the land-grant philosophies. For example, in 1874 a degree program was initiated called Latin Science. A letter from the Farmer's Alliance charged: "We sincerely hope that it is not the intention of the Board of Trustees to . . . introduce Latin again under the specious guise of the Latin Science course."

It was the vision of William Leroy Broun, who was first named president in 1882, that eventually resolved the conflict. His classic scholarship was matched by a love for science and mathematics. Dr. Broun, speaking at Auburn's commencement exercises in 1880, pointed out the South's need for scientific education. During his first year as president, however, he was unable to gain acceptance of his proposed curriculum changes, and he resigned. He was brought back one year later, but during that interval his successor, Dr. David Boyd, had managed to sell those very changes to the board of trustees. Dr. Broun continued as president until his death in 1902. During his tenure, he completely restructured the basic course of study and shaped Auburn's future, with

a balance between the new scientific agricultural program and the traditional cultural curriculum.

In 1899, through the eloquent persuasion of Dr. Broun, the title of the school was officially changed to Alabama Polytechnic Institute. But as noted earlier, Auburn has always been "Auburn" to those who know her intimately. The time finally came to acknowledge that fact and make it official. In 1960, under President Ralph Draughon, the Alabama Polytechnic Institute petitioned to change its name to Auburn University. Presumably that comfortable title will see us into the next millenium.

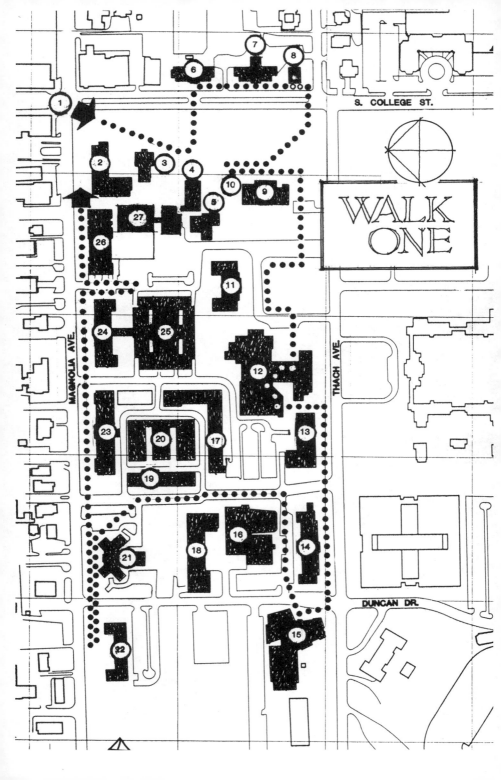

S. COLLEGE ST.

WALK
ONE

MAGNOLIA AVE.

THACH AVE.

DUNCAN DR.

Walk One
The North (Old) Campus

START THIS WALKING TOUR AT THE DOWNTOWN crossroads of College Street and Magnolia Avenue where it all began: Toomer's Corner. These two streets are unofficial boundaries separating campus and town. Except for a few scattered buildings, the Auburn campus has confined itself to the quadrant south of Magnolia and west of College.

This first group includes the oldest and perhaps the richest historically of all campus buildings. There are a few new structures in this section that owe their sites to the sacrifice of earlier landmarks, but Samford Park, the area between Samford and Langdon halls, is the setting for the original East Alabama Male College.

1	Toomer's Corner	15	Pharmacy Building
2	Biggin Hall	16	Broun Hall
3	Hargis Hall	17	L Building
4	Langdon Hall	18	Physical Plant Building
5	Langdon Hall Annex	19	Dunstan Hall
6	Ingram Hall (Alumni Hall)	20	Engineering Shops
7	O. D. Smith Hall	21	Drake Student Health Center
8	University Chapel	22	Noble Hall
9	Samford Hall	23	Textile Building
10	The Lathe	24	Ramsay Hall
11	Ross Hall	25	Wilmore Laboratories
12	Foy Union	26	Harbert Center
13	Tichenor Hall	27	Aerospace Engineering
14	Thach Hall		

[1] TOOMER'S CORNER

While not officially a part of Auburn University, Toomer's Corner is an institution familiar to all campus regulars. It is the juncture where the town of Auburn meets the university of Auburn and must be included in any discussion of the significant landmarks hereabouts. The name comes from Mr. Shel

Toomer, longtime operator of a drug store located across from the historic main gate of the campus. Known for its outstanding limeades—still made according to the original recipe—the drug store has served as a hangout for generations of Auburn students. Alumni return to Toomer's Drug Store to enjoy that sweet, tart, cool drink one more time and to reminisce. Though no longer in the Toomer family, the store is still a drug store after ninety years.

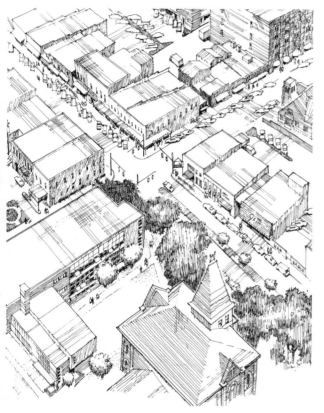

Toomer's Corner marks a sentimental crossroad more than it names a drug store. It is the place where students traditionally let off steam, serious political campaigns are celebrated, and victories in any athletic contest, whether at home or away are made official by the festooning of everything upright with streamers of toilet paper.

Mr. Neil Davis, former owner and editor of the *Auburn Bulletin* and a professor of journalism, wrote often on subjects dear to Auburn fans. One of his accounts examined the reasons for the special significance of this sacrosanct piece of real estate:

The Corner is a landmark made famous by generations of college students who have gathered there after football victories to celebrate and cheer, and for town and gown who turn out there to hear candidates for political office

seek to sell their wares. When Langdon Hall, where the
secessionist firebrand William Lowndes Yancey stirred
Auburnites of 1859–60, grew too small to accommodate
the likes of Big Jim Folsom, political speakers were moved
to Toomer's Corner. Hugo Black, Lister Hill, Folsom, and
George Wallace regularly drew large crowds—sometimes
upward of 2,000 to 3,000—to that spot to hear colorful
oratory of Old South flavor.

Now paved and improved, the intersection of
Magnolia and College bears little resemblance to the
crossroads of old. Most of the businesses in the
immediate neighborhood, including the drug store,
the two oldest banks, and the town's venerable eat-
ing establishments, have undergone facelifts. The
old oaks have yielded to young crape myrtle and the
traffic approaches gridlock at rush hour.

However, as Neil Davis points out, "Although
much has changed on the Plain since the days of
Sheldon Lynne Toomer, the town retains much that
was best in his day and time. Life in Auburn revolves
around Toomer's Corner where much of the history
of the town gets its charac-
ter and flavor. It is Au-
burn's Times Square."

[2] Biggin Hall 1951

The first campus build-
ing one encounters coming
from Toomer's Corner and
downtown Auburn is
Biggin Hall, now home to
the art department. It is a
statement of the new architectural thought coming out
of World War II and generated by European masters
trained at the Bauhaus: a southern version of the International style.

The designers were Pearson, Tittle and Narrows.
Their design included a sun control device on the
west exposure, a set of operable vertical louvers that
could be adjusted with changing sun direction.

Details of this innovation were published in the national journal, *Progressive Architecture*, when the building was built. The louvers are still doing their screening job today, but in a fixed position.

The studio spaces are arranged along the north side, which gives them desirable glare-free, even light. This also puts them in full view of the passing parade along Magnolia Avenue, so the creative efforts of many students are given a continuous impromptu exhibition that everyone seems to enjoy.

The Department of Architecture occupied the building from its beginning until 1977, when the department moved to the new Dudley Hall [54]. A tradition began with the architects and continues today: Biggin Hall is open twenty-four hours a day, seven days a week, and the lights are never turned off.

As head professor of the department, Frederic Child Biggin saw enrollment increase from 11 students in 1916 to 143 in 1943 in architecture, landscape architecture, and interior design. A native New Yorker, Professor Biggin graduated from Cornell in architecture and in mechanical engineering from Lehigh University. He was also the chairman of the Alabama Board of Registration for Architects and a charter member of the Alabama Council, American Institute of Architects.

[3] HARGIS HALL
1888

Constructed initially to serve as the chemistry building, this Romanesque Revival structure with its square tower and semi-circular arched openings occupies a key position in Samford Park, the center of the early campus. The presence of Hargis Hall adds an element of dignity to the front side of the campus. It preceded the construction of Samford Hall [9] by only a few months.

The chemistry department was the principal occupant of the building until the completion of Ross Hall [11] in 1930. At that time, Hargis was remodeled to adapt it for use by the Department of Architecture. Lecture rooms, offices, and the architecture library were on the first floor, while the second floor was used by applied art. In 1951, another remodeling was ordered, this time for the music department, which was attached to the School of Architecture and fine Arts on February 7, 1945. A number of practice rooms were created, and a small auditorium was cut out of the rear portion of the first floor. The sounds of music filled this space for a number of years. Concerts, recitals, band and orchestra rehearsals were all accommodated in Hargis until Goodwin Hall [55], completed in the 1970s, provided the new home for the music department.

At that time, Hargis Hall was once again extensively remodeled for new occupants: the Graduate School, Cooperative Education, and Water Resources Research. A total interior facelift was ordered to transform it into an impressive set of offices and conference spaces with a real sense of elegance.

Before the renovation was completed, however, a fire of unknown origin broke out and completely gutted the interior of the building. All work stopped for nearly a year. The building was cordoned off with wire fencing while insurance settlements and the attorney general's decision on rebidding were worked out. Ironically, the new plans included a sprinkler system and a fire alarm wired directly to the Auburn fire station.

In late 1979, the contractor began again to create a new Hargis Hall inside the shell of the 1880s building. The exterior is little changed except for some missing masonry rosettes that were destroyed in the fire and could not be replaced.

Estes Hargis was a 1917 graduate of Auburn. He went on to earn a medical degree from the University of Pennsylvania and a graduate degree in surgery from the University of Minnesota and the Mayo

Clinic. Dr. Hargis was awarded an honorary degree from Auburn in 1965, following many years of distinguished practice in Birmingham. He and his wife endowed a professorship in English with a gift of $100,000 and contributed another $100,000 toward the latest renovation of Hargis Hall.

[4] LANGDON HALL 1853 *(REBUILT 1883)*

Langdon's history is one of the more colorful of any Auburn landmark. It started life in 1853 on what is now North Gay Street as a chapel for the Auburn Masonic Female College. It was constructed at a cost of $2,500. It soon became the first public meeting hall for the young town and hosted the famous secession debate in the late 1850s. A plaque commemorating this event was placed in Langdon Hall by the United Daughters of the Confederacy in 1914. Dr. Howard Hamell, a member of Auburn's first graduating class after the Civil War, was present at the debate and recalled that unforgettable day in an account written for the April 1914 issue of the *Auburn Alumnus*:

I saw again and again the political princes of the Old South, and you could hardly call one of the greater names of its leaders whom we did not see and hear in Auburn.

The first afternoon speaker was one who never weighed a hundred pounds but was like the 'hammer of Thor' in Southern politics, Alexander H. Stephens. I can see him now as he came to the platform, cigar stump in hand, in loose-fitting clothes ill-kept, with sallow, weazen face that one minute looked like a boy and the next like an old man. Pointing his long thin finger in gesticulation, and speaking in high metallic treble, Stephens held the common people who knew of the desperate battle to greatness he had fought as no other man could hold them. Then came lordly big-brained 'Bob' Toombs of Georgia, owner of great wealth, possessed of great intellect and culture.

Hon. W. P. Brownlow spoke, gaunt, fiery, cutting in satire. I heard him say, "I would rather vote for the old clothes of Henry Clay stuffed with straw than for any living democrat."

At night, after the tide of victory had swept shortly one way and after frantic telegraphic appeals, came Hon. Wm. L. Yancey, pale and sick on a special train from Montgomery, uplifted on the shoulders of men who would have been glad to die for him. For an hour and a half he held the great mob often in a strange pathetic quiet, and then the storm broke forth as I never saw or heard of it under any man in all the great world of oratory.

The wood frame building was acquired by the East Alabama Male College in 1883 and moved to its present site when the women's college closed operations. Nine years later it was totally remodeled and given a distinctive new classic revival look and a brick veneer.

Just before the application of the new brick, the class of 1891 was intent on getting the building painted for graduation. They daubed the exterior with splotches of bright color. One enterprising senior climbed to the front gable and in large letters blocked out the word *PANTE*. This evidence of a lack of scholarship was allowed to remain, greeting students and visitors during the full week of commencement exercises.

During its long history, Langdon Hall has served Auburn in many ways. When Old Main, the predecessor to Samford Hall [9], burned down in 1887, all classes were conducted in Langdon, which was outfitted with temporary partitions. Later, the engineering program, among the first in the South, occupied the ground floor. A wood-working department, established in 1885, was located in half the ground floor, while a machines department occupied the other half until 1887, when the Langdon Hall Annex [5] was completed. The space has served as home to Auburn's first electric dynamo and light plant (1888–1921), the Home Economics Department (1921–24), and the student center. The auditorium also served as a YMCA assembly hall and from 1951 to 1977 accommodated band rehearsals. The auditorium now hosts free movies for students every weekend, and the ground floor is home of the personnel office and stenographic services.

WALK ONE

Charles Langdon was an important figure in Alabama politics in the late 1800s. He was the mayor of Mobile, a state legislator for several terms, a member of the Constitutional Conventions of 1865 and 1875, and secretary of state from 1885 to 1889. In 1865, Colonel Langdon was elected to Congress, but his seat was denied him. Having served many years as an Auburn trustee, he was honored by his fellow trustees at the time of his death by having this pivotal campus building named for him.

[5] LANGDON HALL ANNEX 1905

Over the years, there have been a number of buildings labeled Langdon Annex. However, the records indicate this is the Langdon Annex that initially served electric powerhouse machinery and steam and electrical labs. On the second floor was a pattern and wood-turning shop. Later, this building was known as the Music Annex, in the days when Hargis Hall [3] housed the music department and Langdon [4] was the rehearsal hall for the band.

The Beaux Arts structure, with its arched window and door openings and brick detailing, bears a family

resemblance to Samford [9] and Hargis halls, but shows a bit more restraint. A three-story building, or two stories with a generous attic hidden behind a concave mansard roof, the Annex has always been a faithful servant but never a star. It now houses adjunct offices serving the administration.

The area in front of Langdon Annex, just off the fast lane of student traffic, has been turned into a landscaped oasis. It is an excellent place to pause on the tour. At a lower level, it forms an intimate and sheltered outdoor room walled with banks of azaleas, mondo grass, and flowering plants. Dedicated to Annie Terrell Basore by Chi Omega Sorority for whom she was alumnae adviser for thirty years, it celebrates sixty years on campus for that Greek organization.

[6] INGRAM HALL (ALUMNI HALL) 1923

The building known for years as Alumni Hall was renamed and totally renovated in 1988. Originally serving as a fifty-three room dormitory for men, the first renovation in 1953 converted it to a women's dormitory. In 1975, it was renovated again and designated as a residence for freshman women. At that time, all entering female students were required to be housed in supervised University domiciles.

The Georgian building was designed by Warren, Knight and Davis, who were architects for many University structures during the 1920s. It has a three-story entrance capped with a gabled roof. The latest renovation added a pair of high walls, curving into the entry, further reinforcing the symmetry and, incidentally, concealing a ramp for handicapped users.

The original dormitory building included the unusual amenity of a swimming pool in the basement. This was sacrificed during an earlier renovation when it was filled in to provide space for the alumni dining hall.

The latest renovation provided more space for an expanding college administration. The Office of Business and finance moved into Ingram Hall after an official renaming ceremony on May 6, 1988. The $1.5-million overhaul made twenty-five thousand square feet of office space on four floors available for the controller, financial information systems, payroll and employee benefits, purchasing, financial reporting, budget control, accounts payable, and external auditors.

William Travis Ingram compiled one of the longest records of continuous service to Auburn University so far recorded. An Opelika native, he joined the University as an auditor in 1925 and retired some forty-eight years later as business manager and treasurer. Besides serving as Auburn's chief financial officer, Mr. Ingram was treasurer of the Alumni Association for twenty-eight years, president of the Auburn City Council for four years, a charter member of the Auburn Lion's Club, and a member of the board of stewards of the Methodist church for twenty-four years.

[7] O. D. SMITH HALL 1908 *(REBUILT 1934)*

O. D. Smith Hall serves today as home and headquarters for the industrial design department. When it was built there were no industrial designers at Auburn; in fact, there was no industrial design profession. This classic building in the flemish style, designed by architects Warren and Walton, has served many masters and accommodated a great variety of functions. It serves as a testimonial to the flexibility of the classic facade and its ability to lend a measure of dignity to whatever is contained therein.

The porch is grandly proportioned, with four Ionic columns and regal cartouches set in the wall to give great importance to the front entry. The deep windows on the first floor are given an elegant framing through the use of an oversized brick arch and a diamond

ceramic tile insert centered over the top. The brick-
work is flemish bond, alternating dark burned half
bricks with full bricks in Auburn red.

Originally intended as a dormitory for men, it
temporarily became a hospital in 1918 for students
suffering from the killer swine flu. In 1921, it was
converted to a dormitory for women. Fire struck
the building on Thanksgiving Day 1933, and the
thirty-four women residents were suddenly without a
home. Townspeople and other students found space
and donated funds and services for the displaced
girls so they could finish the academic year. A grant
from the Civilian Works Administration and funds
from the insurance company made it possible for the
University to rebuild O. D. Smith Hall within the un-
damaged outside walls, but this time as a classroom
and laboratory facility for the School of Home Economics. An annex for home economics research was
added in 1948 on property negotiated from the Presbyterian church.

The art department fell heir to O. D. Smith when
home economics built its larger facility, Spidle Hall
[34], in 1962. Art soon outgrew the building and was
moved across the street to Biggin Hall [2] when that
space became available. Industrial design, enjoying
its new status as an autonomous department, took
possession of O. D. Smith Hall in 1980. Its next re-
incarnation will no doubt be as an administration
building.

Otis David Smith was one of Auburn's early
leaders, coming to Alabama in 1854. He served as
principal of schools at Smith's Station and Opelika
and joined the Auburn faculty as professor of English in 1873. He served as chairman of mathematics
from 1874 to 1904 and as acting president in 1902.
He had the distinction of serving on The University
of Alabama's board of trustees while a professor at
Auburn. He was, in fact, awarded an honorary Doctor of Laws degree by The University of Alabama, a
rare example of institutional largesse between these
two state rivals.

WALK ONE

[8] UNIVERSITY CHAPEL 1850

The Chapel is the oldest building still on its original site and still in use by the University. It was built as a Presbyterian church by slaves belonging to Edwin Reese, one of Auburn's first residents, on a lot donated by Judge John Harper, who founded the town of Auburn in 1836. Mr. Reese prepared all of the materials necessary for construction of the building on his plantation, including burning lime to make the brick.

In 1852, the first communion services were held in the church. They were conducted by Edwin Reese's mother, Anna. Two of the early pastors were Dr. George Petrie, the father of Dean George Petrie, and George Maxton, professor of English literature at Auburn.

There is some confusion about just when the college acquired the church. Sam Brewster, longtime director of buildings and grounds, records the date as 1900. Other sources claim it was 1921 and that the building was traded by the Presbyterians for the lot where their present church now stands, with the stipulation that the old building not be destroyed. Either way, the Chapel has a colorful past, having served variously as a Civil War hospital, a civic center, the Y-Hut (a YMCA and YWCA headquarters), a USO, a temporary classroom and, for forty years, as the playhouse for the Department of Theatre. It has now come full circle and again serves as a chapel, fulfilling a need for the campus that had been recognized and discussed for years.

Through contributions from a number of sources the Chapel was given an imaginative restoration in 1976 and designated a bicentennial building in the National Register of Historic Buildings. Professor of Architecture Nicholas Davis was responsible for the sensitive rebuilding.

In the beginning, the church had a Greek Revival front porch with two front doors, one for men and one for women. The building was Gothicized with a corner entrance and steeple in the early 1900s. The interior ceiling was flat, beaded wood planking,

typical of the late nineteenth century. When these
mostly rotten planks were removed in the last renovation, the hand-sawn, mortised and pegged beams
were thought to be much handsomer than the ceiling
and were left exposed.

The surrounding courtyards define the church yard, form outdoor gathering places, and reduce traffic noise. The rounded front court encompasses passing pedestrians, inviting them to pause on sheltered benches and enjoy the walled gardens. These walls were not a part of the original building, but streets were quieter and narrower then.

The building is open from 8 A.M. to 6 P.M. weekdays. A colorful sequence of banners displaying religious symbols from many faiths hangs from the rough hewn beams and trusses. Each religious organization on campus submitted the design for its own banner, and students from the Department of Consumer Affairs hand-sewed each of them. To meet the great variety of multi-faith liturgical needs, a flexible system allows the banners to be hung in any location on the beams. The cross can also be removed from the altar and replaced by a banner.

Without the creative leadership of President Harry Philpot and Academic Vice-President Taylor Littleton, who shepherded the restoration, many of the inspired features would have been cut from the budget.

[9] SAMFORD HALL 1888

The original building on this site, the first structure serving the East Alabama Male College, was erected in 1859. Being the only building and housing all functions of the embryo school, it was tagged The Old Main. The architect was a famous Philadelphian, Steven Decatur Button, who also designed the ill-fated Montgomery statehouse in 1846.

After a fire on June 24, 1887, left only a pile of scorched bricks and some charred timbers, it was rumored that the loss might be the end of the school. But President Broun issued notice that Auburn would open as usual in the fall. And it did. Langdon Hall [4], the second campus building, was partitioned into classrooms and the chapel became a temporary lecture hall.

Bricks from Old Main helped form the foundation for the new building to be erected on the same

site. The building was designed by Bruce and Morgan. That firm was one of the best known architectural offices in the Southeast at a time when America was in its "city beautiful" mood. They were responsible for dozens of exuberant courthouses, city halls, depots, libraries, banks, and churches, in a range of popular styles: High Victorian Gothic, Queen Anne, Renaissance, Romanesque, and Second Empire Revivalist, which describes Samford Hall. It is a prototypical land-grant college building featuring multiple gables, brick richly ornamented with stone, terra cotta decoration, and a tall clock tower. Georgia Tech's administration building by the same firm is another example.

In Auburn's early days, Samford Hall was the college. With the exception of Langdon Hall, which served as chapel and auditorium, all academic activity, including the library, centered in Samford. Instruction was given in all disciplines in the classrooms of Samford, and all faculty and administrative offices were here. It was 1969 before Samford Hall was without the sound of students passing into and out of the building on the hour. The building was totally remodeled at that time to serve as offices for the president and the central administration.

The bell in Samford tower served a very real purpose in those early years. The students called it Big Ben. They were awakened by its persuasive pealing, which summoned them to mandatory chapel services at an early hour each day. The bell also announced the changing of classes. But the four faces often failed to agree on the time, so students could pick the most convenient reading for their particular purpose.

The bell was silent for many years until, in 1939, President Duncan climbed the steep belfry stairs and pulled the rope to signal the start of Greater Auburn Day and a $1.5-million building program. The original clock was ordered from the Lux Thomas Clock Company in Thomaston, Connecticut. The bell was cast in 1889 in Troy, New York, by Clinton Meneely Bell Company. It weighs 4,200 pounds and is inscribed with its birthdate and the name Alabama

Polytechnic Institute. The climb to the tower winds through the attic and up rickety stairs into the loft. The route is peppered with the carved initials of young lovers and nicknames of students from another time.

A tall tale still rumored on campus has it that several mischievous students and an unwilling cow made the trip into the bell tower back in the 1920s. The cow didn't object to climbing the steep stairs, but she was not easily persuaded to walk back down.

Samford Hall was officially named for William James Samford in May 1929. Governor Samford attended Auburn in 1860–61 and the University of Georgia in 1861–62. After the Civil War he studied law, served in the Alabama state legislature, in Congress, and as a delegate to the Constitutional Convention of 1875. His term as governor of Alabama was cut short by his death at age fifty-seven in 1901.

The name Samford has been closely associated with Auburn throughout its history. A family member has served on the board of trustees for seventy-seven years of this century. William James Samford, Jr., a 1972 Auburn graduate in political science and great-grandson of the governor Samford, is today's family representative.

[10] THE LATHE 1862

Just off the northeast corner of Samford Hall [9] stands an unusual artifact that marks a significant event in the history of Alabama and the nation—the Civil War. Though an unconventional monument, nothing could more effectively symbolize the struggle and suffering that the nation, and most especially the South, went through during those difficult years.

The powerful form can also be interpreted as a symbol of another happening at Auburn: the advent of the industrial age, which precipitated a change in the fundamental direction of the University, a shift from classical studies to a greater concentration on the mechanical arts and scientific pursuits.

Donated to the University in 1936, the Lathe was

formally set in place by Alpha Phi Omega in 1952. Its story, as recorded on the plaque mounted at the base, is an interesting one.

Built in Selma, Alabama, during the early part of the civil war for the manufacture of military supplies for the Confederate Army. During the war an attempt was made to move it to Columbus, Georgia, to prevent its being seized by Federal Troops. Enroute, it was buried for a time near Irondale, Alabama. When the danger of capture had passed, it was dug up and moved to Columbus, where it was used for boring cannon until the end of the war. After the war the lathe was used by the Birmingham rolling mills which later became part of the Tennessee Coal Iron and Railroad Company. In 1936 that company presented this historic lathe to the Alabama Polytechnic Institute.

[11] ROSS HALL 1930

Ross Hall is a handsome Georgian style building occupying a key position in this central campus complex. It presents a symmetrical facade to the formal landscaped gardens that are flanked by Samford Hall [9] on the east and Foy Union [12] on the west. This is Ross Square, Auburn's formal front door.

The careful attention to style in the design of the exterior envelope by Warren, Knight and Davis rather denies the no-nonsense laboratory function of the building. For ease of maintenance and remodeling, all piping was left exposed, and there were seventeen fans to remove fumes.

The building was constructed in just one year, a feat that would be hard to match today even with the sophisticated construction equipment now available.

President Bradford Knapp and Professor Bennett Ross turned the first shovelsful of soil in a ceremony on April 30, 1929, and the School of Chemistry moved into the structure in March 1930.

Professor Ross died April 4, 1930, just as the work was completed. One of the first uses of the building was as a sanctuary for the distinguished chemist to lie in state. The casket, banked with flowers, was displayed in the main corridor, and the office that was to have been occupied by Professor Ross was draped in black. His shrouded photograph was positioned on his desk. He was sixty-six.

So, this man who had served Auburn in many ways—as professor of chemistry, dean of agricultural science, dean of chemistry and pharmacy, and twice as acting president—was honored in this dramatic way. And the laboratory building that he helped to shape serves as a memorial to his life.

In 1964, the School of Chemistry moved out of Ross Hall into Saunders Laboratory [53]. Ross Hall was renovated in 1977 for the use of mechanical, chemical, and aerospace engineering.

[12] FOY UNION 1953

The original building was funded by the students, who voted to assess themselves through an increase in fees over a period of years. Designed by Pearson, Tittle and Narrows in a contemporary International style, it was expanded sympathetically in 1972 by the same firm. That addition forced the removal of

the handsome old alumni gym to make space available on the west side.

The Union serves as a home away from home for Auburn students and is the center for nearly all student organizations on campus. The central campus information desk is here, and one can get the final word on scheduled events, ballgame scores, and changes in meeting rooms and times.

Other offerings are the Union Ballroom, Spectra Recreation Room, a reading room, a gallery, administrative offices, and the War Eagle cafeteria, which is the main attraction for most students. It is also open to the public.

James E. Foy served as dean of student affairs from 1950 until his retirement in 1978. He and Katharine Cater, who was dean of women, took on

matching roles as the custodians and cultivators of
the Auburn Spirit, that pervasive feeling of being a
part of a continuing tradition that is shared by generations of students. Jim Foy's bouncy personality and
upbeat attitude were as dependable as the morning
sunrise. He retired in 1978 to join Governor Fob
James's administration in Montgomery. (Fob was an
Auburn graduate and football star.)

[13] TICHENOR HALL 1940

Tichenor Hall was built just before the interruption
of all building activity imposed by World War II. It
was known for many years as the New Classroom
Building before being named for Auburn's third
president. Tichenor represents one of the purest examples of Georgian architecture on the campus.

Its symmetrical front facade is enlivened with three
balanced gables, a stonefaced base platform, and
quoined stone corners. The Georgian style, a phase
of English Renaissance, was named for the four
Georges who reigned consecutively as English mon-
archs between 1714 and 1830.

Before assuming Auburn's presidency in 1872,
Isaac Taylor Tichenor was a chaplain in the Confederate army and a pastor of the first Baptist Church in

Memphis. Under his guidance, Auburn evolved from a denominational liberal arts school to a state-supported land-grant college. He had a vision of a new educational direction that would influence the development of agriculture and harness Alabama's immense resources to improve the condition of her people. Dr. Tichenor left office in 1882 with his plan well established, and subsequent years have proved the legitimacy of that new direction for the school and for the state.

The College of Business now occupies Tichenor, as well as Thach Hall [14], and the concerns of the business faculty for the economic health of Alabama and the region would coincide with Dr. Tichenor's vision of 1872.

[14] THACH HALL 1951

In his *General History of Campus Construction at Auburn University*, Sam Brewster, the former director of buildings and grounds, classified this building as Contemporary Georgian. And that may be as precise a label as can be put on it. The simplified bold forms stripped of all ornament were a popular style

of the early 1950s. The building, designed by Van Keuren, Davis, was known as the General Education Building in its early years. Its accommodations for thirty-nine offices, twenty-four classrooms and laboratories, a small auditorium, and a conference room now serve the College of Business.

Charles C. Thach served as Auburn's sixth president (1902–

WALK ONE

20) after twenty years as professor of English and political economy. His feelings about the college were summed up in this quotation reported in *Lengthening Shadows*: "the Alabama Polytechnic Institute to be a high sounding phrase . . . fit for legal documents and grave legislation, but not to conjure with and not to yell and not to dream with as is 'Fair Auburn.'" The marked progress made during his administration he attributed to that creative force—intangible, but nonetheless real—called Auburn Spirit.

[15] PHARMACY BUILDING 1975

This expressive contemporary building designed by Blondheim, Williams and Chancey stands almost defiantly among its more classically restrained academic neighbors. Internal functions have been encouraged to express themselves, so that one may read something of the internal goings-on through the forms that make up the building masses. An auditorium lecture hall projects into the intersection, exhaust ducts carry foul fumes beyond the roof, and a glassy greenhouse shows off its proliferating product in an appendage. This is an extrovert in the society of classic academic red brick blocks.

Pharmacy instruction at Auburn began in 1885. The department became a school in 1941 and was housed in Miller Hall [77] from 1952. The new building reflects a changing perspective of pharmacy as a discipline that helps ensure safety and ethics in medical practice and provides total health care services far beyond old-fashioned corner drug store operations. It also reflects expansion into a doctoral program that has its own wing of the building for graduate and research studies.

[16] BROUN HALL 1983

The construction of Broun Hall represents the first step in the master plan for creation of the new complex of buildings to serve the College of Engineering. It was Building I. Ground-breaking ceremonies were held on April 30, 1982, after a lengthy delay generated by high interest rates prevalent for a time. The cost was $6 million, nearly equal to the price of Auburn's enormous Haley Center [40], built fourteen years earlier.

Broun Hall is home to the electrical engineering department. It contains sixteen classrooms, thirty-five laboratories, offices for administration, faculty, staff, and graduate students, a three-hundred seat auditorium, and a study room. The red brick was chosen to mirror the treatment of the Pharmacy Building [15] and Haley Center. As part of a larger master plan, two landscaped brick walkways, or malls, form a cohesive connection to the immediate neighborhood and the rest of campus.

Your route takes you past the south end of Broun, where you will see evidence of an ongoing research project reflecting our perpetual search for a supply of clean energy. Collector panels angled toward the sun are turning solar energy into electrical energy—enough, in this case, to keep fifty-seven 100-watt lightbulbs burning forever.

Broun Hall honors William Leroy Broun, Auburn's fourth president (1882–83 and 1884–1902). It is the second building on campus to have been labeled Broun Hall. The first was razed in 1984 to make way for Harbert Center [26] as part of the expansion and upgrading of the engineering complex. According to *Lengthening Shadows*, during President Broun's long tenure Auburn was brought "to the forefront of scientific institutions, equipping it for teaching the sciences and their application to the economic needs of the South." Bright young teachers were invited to join the faculty, women were admitted, and football was introduced.

[17] L BUILDING 1923

Rather undistinguished architecturally, this building derives its name from its shape. Funds and materials for the original building were donated, and the actual cost to the University was just $1,500. A wing added in 1929 gave the building its L shape. The original east wing was demolished in 1948 to accommodate the Wilmore Laboratories [25]. The building has been used for many purposes over the years; since 1975 it has been a computer center for engineering students.

[18] PHYSICAL PLANT BUILDING 1950

The Department of Buildings and Grounds was organized in 1940 by Sam Brewster, who was named its first director. The wide-ranging operations of the department were pulled together with the construction of this L-shaped building in 1950.

The greatly expanded work of maintenance and construction for the entire campus is now carried out by the Department of Physical Plant. The department is housed in new quarters (not included on the tour) in the wide open spaces of West Samford Avenue.

[19] DUNSTAN HALL 1959

Formerly occupied by electrical engineering, the building is now home to the industrial engineering department and the computer science and engineering department. Its laboratories are invariably populated with red-eyed students intently monitoring computer screens. The building has obligingly accommodated a new technology that could not have been anticipated when it was constructed.

Arthur St. Charles Dunstan was head professor of electrical engineering (1899–1951) and physics (1899–1903 and 1914–19). During this remarkable period of service, Professor Dunstan found time to develop an electroscope, which he used for radium hunting and which earned him significant national recognition.

[20] Engineering Shops 1941

With the aid of federal funds, these three buildings were constructed by National Youth Administration boys for use as industrial shops. The college took them over in 1944.

[21] Drake Student Health Center 1939

Recognized as a necessary adjunct service to the student body, the first medical facilities were added to the campus scene in 1931. The Glenn House on Mell Street was converted to an infirmary with eight beds and an isolation room for students with contagious diseases.

The need for larger and updated infirmary facilities soon became clear. After a temporary move to

the east wing of old Broun Hall, construction was
started in 1938 from a design by Warren, Knight and

Davis. With its central gabled entry, cupola, and quoined brick corners, Drake is a Georgian building with a difference. The two end wings, angled at forty-five degrees, offer a symbolic gesture of comfort and welcome to those in need of the services offered within. In 1977, a badly needed addition was added to expand the range of services and bring the capacity to fifty-four beds.

John Hodges Drake was the college surgeon from 1873 until his death in 1926, a remarkable fifty-three-year record. It is reported that, until shortly before his death, he never missed a day from his office. He enlisted in the Confederate army at age sixteen and served as drummer boy in Company A, fifty-third Alabama Mounted Infantry. He earned his medical degree from Georgia Medical College in 1867.

[22] NOBLE HALL 1957

Built to house men only, the dormitory now has both male and female residents, illustrating the changing times. Men and women are housed in separate wings, in about equal numbers, and all in double rooms.

The hall gets its name from Auburn graduate Robert Noble, who served with distinction in the Medical Corps in Panama, the Philippines, Puerto Rico, Ecuador, and Africa. In retirement, Major General Noble rendered monumental service to Auburn, his community, and his country.

Noble Hall is the only surviving member of the old residence hall complex on Magnolia Avenue.

Bullard and its twin neighbor, Magnolia Hall, were the victims of natural wear and tear. They were demolished in 1987. Their removal made way for the new $15-million home for the College of Business, which is under construction at the time of this writing.

23] TEXTILE BUILDING 1932

Built under the cloud of the Great Depression, the Textile Building was creatively financed through the sale of University-owned electric and water franchises. That sale, which netted $300,000 on an original investment of $125,000, helped President Bradford Knapp (1928–32) realize a portion of his ambitious capital improvement program during those difficult times. A number of other proposed facilities had to be abandoned.

The Flemish bond brick coursing done in two colors, an Auburn red alternating with a dark burned half brick and separated by wide off-white mortar joints, seems to suggest the warp and woof of a textured fabric. However, since the same pattern was used on Ramsay Hall [24], Textile's neighbor to the east, it is unlikely that the effect was a conscious intent by the designers, Warren, Knight and Davis. The two buildings are closely matched in basic institutional Georgian style despite their one-story difference in height. Each has a symmetrical three-gable front facade, with cut stone enhancement of the central entry celebrated with a stone cartouche.

In the central lobby are several deep glass-front display cabinets, which southeastern textile manufacturers have been invited to fill with samples of their current products. These displays serve to remind students of the strong ties to an important regional industry. Visitors may also enjoy these colorful presentations. The laboratories at either end of the first floor are alive with the intricate and complex machinery employed in the textile industry.

[24] RAMSAY HALL 1925

Ramsay Hall presents a statement of obvious importance on Magnolia Avenue. Its Neoclassic Georgian front and crowning cupola carry an air of authority signifying the primary headquarters of the College of Engineering. The building houses the office of the dean, many of the engineering faculty, pre-engineering programs, laboratories, the engineering extension service, and the engineering experiment station. Ramsay Hall, with its forty-three offices and laboratories, was the School of Engineering for many years until the pressure of enrollment and the growing reputation of the school mandated the addition of new facilities.

Prior to Ramsay's construction, the building that housed the beginnings of the School of Veterinary Medicine stood on this site. It was a pharmacy and instrument building and was relocated down Magnolia Avenue opposite Drake Student Health Center [21]. Later remodeled as a fraternity house, it eventually became a private residence.

Erskine Ramsay, for whom the building is named, was a Pennsylvania native, a mining engineer, and an adopted son of the state of Alabama. He held patents on some forty inventions for devices he had developed to make the extraction of coal from the earth a faster and easier process. He was awarded the William Laurence Saunders Gold Medal of the American Institute of Mining and Metallurgical Engineers.

WALK ONE

Mr. Ramsay was a man who enjoyed being busy. He held the title of president of two coal companies

and vice-president of two others. At the same time, he served as an officer or director of a number of Alabama's leading manufacturing, financial, and mercantile enterprises.

Mr. Ramsay's contribution of $100,000 in 1924 began the fund to construct the building. Designed by Warren, Knight and Davis, it was erected at a total cost of $250,000. A dedication ceremony was held in Langdon Hall [4] on October 10, 1925. Victor Hanson of the *Birmingham News* presided.

[25] WILMORE LABORATORIES 1949

Another building in the Georgian style, which predominates among the older buildings on campus,

Wilmore Laboratories was designed by Sizemore and Campbell. It stands in the heart of the engineering complex, almost hidden from the view of the outsider, and plays an important

servant role. Here, theories are tested, hypotheses are turned into reality, and the hard work of experimentation and discovery is conducted.

John Jenkins Wilmore spent more than half a century in creative exploration at Auburn. He arrived as an instructor of civil engineering in 1888, then served concurrently as professor of mechanical engineering and dean of engineering from 1889 to 1943. He served as chairman of the administrative committee of three that conducted the affairs of the University in lieu of a president from 1932 to 1935 and helped Auburn through some difficult years of the Depression.

Professor Wilmore built a steam engine in 1889 to generate electricity for lights in Langdon Hall [4] and Old Main (now the site of Samford Hall [9]), the first college buildings in the South to enjoy that particular kind of enlightenment. He was also instrumental in 1924 in developing a source of water for Auburn that was appropriately named Lake Wilmore.

[26] HARBERT CENTER 1986

Harbert Center represents the second major building to be added to the engineering complex as part of the 1980s campaign to upgrade facilities of the School of Engineering. (Broun Hall [16] for electrical engineering was Building I.) The very serious needs of the School (now College) of Engineering were brought to light in a study by a private planning consultant in 1979. According to the consultant, existing facilities were "about half that required to support the present curriculum." Engineering needs were included in a major fund raising campaign launched in 1982. Titled the Auburn University Generations Fund, its overall goal was $61.7 million.

Alumni will remember another building on this site. Old Broun Hall was a prominent Auburn landmark from 1906 to 1984. It originally provided space for the Departments of Engineering and Mining, but later served a great variety of departmental occupants, finally becoming home to the ROTC

WALK ONE

programs on campus. The announcement that Broun Hall would be razed to make way for a new facility brought forth a hue and cry from alumni, faculty, and others who felt a significant piece of the Auburn fabric was being thrown away in the name of progress. To partially ameliorate these concerns, a recognizable and prominent feature from Broun was salvaged and stored, waiting for the day it could be reused. The four stone columns and pediment that marked the main entrance to Broun now form an impressive portico entry for the Nichols Center [74].

The John M. Harbert III Civil Engineering Center is both a teaching facility and a research laboratory, with environmental isolation rooms and a reaction floor, as well as classrooms and office space. It was designed by Auburn alumnus Harry Goleman of Goleman and Rolfe, Associates, Inc. The Center was named for its chief benefactor, Auburn graduate and corporate executive, whose $5 million gift made it possible.

The center qualifies as Postmodern in style, with a number of quotations from traditional forms and repeats of gabled roofs and architectural elements from nearby campus buildings. A rather elegant, imposing presence on campus, its exterior appearance somewhat belies the bare bones utility of the cavernous laboratory spaces inside.

[27] Aerospace Engineering 1990

The Department of Aerospace Engineering will finally enjoy its own facility, designed to meet its special requirements, when construction is

completed in the spring of 1991. The site is behind
Harbert Center [26] where the balance of the engineering complex is destined to be situated. The only
remaining piece in the master plan will be a building
for chemical engineering. It has not yet been funded.

Architects for Aerospace Engineering and the
shared classroom building that will be attached are
Goleman and Rolfe, the architects of the Harbert
Center and the firm that developed the engineering
master plan. They will complete the complex to
ensure a sense of consistent and compatible design
character.

WALK ONE

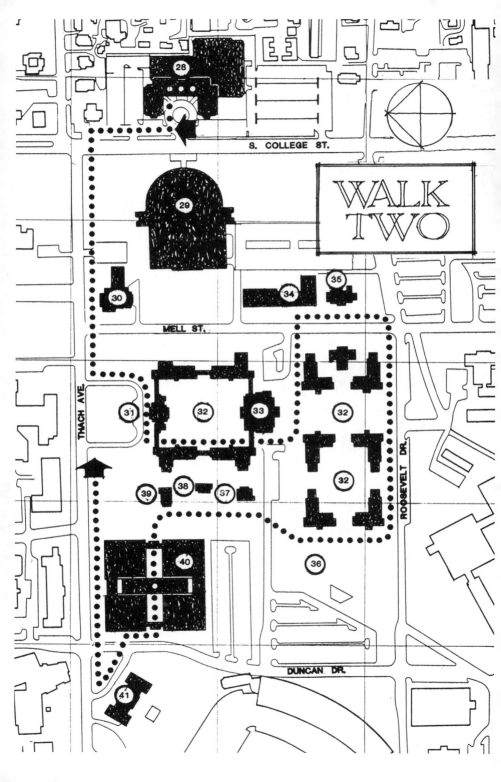

S. COLLEGE ST.

WALK
TWO

MELL ST.

THACH AVE.

ROOSEVELT DR.

DUNCAN DR.

Walk Two
The Central (Second Generation) Campus

START THIS WALKING TOUR AT THE HOTEL AND CON-
ference Center, Auburn's prestigious new
building on South College Street. After you
have seen its up-beat Postmodern interior spaces,
cross College Street (carefully) to the core of the
campus.

This is the Campus Martius, the area that absorbed
campus expansion when steady increase in enrollment forced the boundaries of the fledgling college
out of the confines of Samford Park. It is now a
mixed-use arena containing the newly enlarged main
library, one of the country's largest football stadiums,
and the campus's largest academic building. There is
also a sizable dormitory complex, which encloses a
handsome outdoor space within its double quadran-
gular plan.

28 Hotel and Conference
   Center
29 Draughon Library
30 Mary Martin Hall
31 The Social Center
   (Cater Hall)
32 Women's Quadrangles
33 The Quad Center
34 Spidle Hall

35 Mell Hall
36 The Aviary
37 Human Sciences
   Annex
38 Glanton House
39 Child Study Center
40 Haley Center
41 Petrie Hall

[28] Hotel and Conference Center 1988

This imposing facility was part of a long-range
plan that James Martin brought with him when he
was recruited from the University of Arkansas to become Auburn's fourteenth president. Announced
in 1985, the project went through a series of delays
after the site had been cleared. Four fraternity houses,
Phi Delta Theta, Delta Sigma Phi, Pi Kappa Phi, and
Alpha Gamma Rho, had to be razed to provide the

five-acre site in the heart of the campus. A settlement was negotiated with each of them, along with a lease on a new site on University land.

Ground was broken on January 26, 1987, with Governor Guy Hunt in attendance. The first scheduled conference in the center began on August 15, 1988, when the National Asphalt Pavement Association came to town for a two-day meeting. The Center's official opening was on September 30.

This facility represents a commitment on the part of the University to its mission in extension. The hotel and the conference center are separate entities under different management arrangements. Two hundred forty-nine guest rooms, a lounge, restaurant, delicatessen, and gift shop make up the hotel. The conference center advertises "a large ballroom and junior ballroom, an auditorium, seminar room, computer lab and board room, plus eight meeting rooms." All are served by state-of-the-art audio-visual equipment.

Architecturally, the building may best be described as Postmodern. The term suggests the recall of traditional forms, a symmetrical organization, and a strongly articulated central axis. The ground floor presents a solid base penetrated by a series of arched openings and reinforced by a number of continuous projecting brick moldings of contrasting color. The building is capped by the strong expression of the top floor, with more stripes of the lighter brick and a change in fenestration. The dark tinted glass used to cut heat transmission on a vulnerable west exposure

is somewhat ominous from the exterior. It is relieved, however, when the sun goes down and the
night-lighting gives a new look to downtown Auburn
after dark.

The University owns the land. The Algernon Blair
Group owns the building and manages the hotel, and
Auburn has leased back and operates the conference
center. The facilities can be booked by any group
through the sales and marketing staff.

[29] DRAUGHON LIBRARY 1963

The completion of this new facility dramatically
projected Auburn into a new dimension; it represented a major upward shift in the University's status
as an institution of higher learning. The building

dwarfs the former library building, Mary Martin Hall
[30]. Its four floors, basement, and sub-basement
contained 172,000 square feet, had a design capacity
of 1 million vol-
umes and could ac-
commodate twelve
hundred readers at
one time.

However, when
the collection grew
to 1.5 million
volumes, over-
flowing shelves and
crowding reading
and working areas,

need for expansion became undeniable. The $20.5-million addition was completed in the spring of 1990, increasing floor space to nearly 400,000 square feet and seating to two thousand, and providing the University's first parking deck, with space for 345 cars.

Architects were Pearson, Humphries and Jones. Construction was by Harbert International.

The new addition presents a half-circular front facade facing College Street and nearly on axis with the new Conference Center [28] across the street. Together, the two building forms create a symbolic new gateway to the campus.

Ralph Brown Draughon was Auburn's tenth president (1947–1965), a period of significant growth following World War II. Dr. Draughon was the third alumnus to be honored with the presidency. He had been a member of Auburn's history department since 1931, then director of instruction under President Duncan. When he left office in 1965, President Draughon had awarded 27,457 degrees. Contrasting that with the 16,304 degrees granted at Auburn in the ninety years prior to his tenure, we get a sense of the accelerating rate of change—a change that continues today.

[30] MARY MARTIN HALL 1910

Originally serving as, and called, the Main Library, the building was financed with a generous gift from Andrew Carnegie and an endowment raised by the University, much of which was donated by Auburn citizens. Since that time, the townspeople have had free access to the University library. It was built on what was then called Faculty Avenue on the site of Professor P. H. Mell's home. In addition to his financial help, Carnegie made another contribution to the library: his collection of Thomas Campbell's poems. Carnegie's personal interest in Auburn was due to a conversation he had with Professor J. R. Rutland. The nature of their meeting was not recorded, but the professor must have made a strong impression.

Well-proportioned, imposing, and dignified, Mary Martin Hall is one of the best examples of classical Renaissance architecture on campus. Its human scale and welcoming demeanor belie the fact that it is a four-story building. It was one of the first buildings on campus to be lighted by electricity and heated by steam. Its present function unfortunately dictates that the interior be fragmented into small rooms and corridors.

Mary Eugenia Martin was Auburn's librarian from 1918 to 1949. She was twice president of the Alabama Library Association, a campaigner for extended library facilities in Alabama, and a principal in the development of the county library system.

Originally several life-sized reproductions of classical statues were placed in the library to give a touch of class to the building. Some of the women in town, however, were shocked by the lack of drapery on certain of the voluptuous figures. They took it upon themselves to dress the statues in yellow, pleated silk kilts. There is no report of what eventually happened to the cast statues or their kilts.

Martin Hall served as the University library until the completion of the Ralph Brown Draughon Library [29] in January 1963. By 1912, Martin Hall housed 15,000 books; today, the University's collection exceeds 1.5 million volumes. The change parallels the growth in enrollment and the increase in prestige and support enjoyed by the University.

The building was renovated for administrative office use in 1964 and now houses the registrar, student services, financial aid, and student affairs offices.

[31] THE SOCIAL CENTER (CATER HALL) 1915

This building was constructed to serve as home for the University's chief executive officer, the president. The stately, two-storied, Neoclassic style building was designed by Joseph Hudnut, a member of the architecture faculty who later became dean of the Graduate School of Design at Harvard. The cost was $17,000.

Dr. Charles Thach (1902–20) was the first president to occupy the new home. According to historians, he was pressed to complete a nursery for the birth of his granddaughter, Nellie Thach Curtis, daughter of Bessie and Courtland Curtis. The baby was born in the mansion on August 15, 1915.

Successive presidents living here were Dr. Spright Dowell (1920–28), Dr. Bradford Knapp (1928–32), and Dr. Luther Noble Duncan (1935–47). Dr. Duncan moved out of the house in 1938 to take up residence in the newly completed President's Home [61] on Mell Street, which continues to serve Auburn presidents.

Since 1938, Cater Hall has functioned as office

and home for deans of women and various members of their staffs. It was remodeled in 1940 as the Social Center, with upstairs living quarters for the dean of women. At each end of the building were dating parlors—little cubicles without doors, which the students referred to as mushrooms—where women could entertain their dates.

The Social Center came into full bloom when

Katharine Cooper Cater became dean of women in 1946. She made it the setting for countless teas, coffees, receptions, meetings, and student parties. Dean Cater instituted a reception for senior women each spring and fall, and her annual Christmas party for students, faculty, and townspeople grew each year until it included hundreds of guests.

Katharine Cater was named dean at Auburn after serving as an English teacher at Limestone College and director of student personnel at Furman College. In 1976, with the newly sensitized issue of equality between the sexes, her title was changed to dean of student life. Her devotion to Auburn and her generous outpouring of love and assistance to Auburn students made Katharine Cater a legend during her lifetime. She was stricken with cancer and died in 1980, just five months after the building was named for her.

[32] WOMEN'S QUADRANGLES 1940, 1952

This group of women's dormitories was built in two phases. The first four were started in 1938 with help from President Roosevelt's Public Works Administration program. The second group was built in 1952. The upper quadrangle, dorms I through IV, was dedicated on May 3, 1940, with an address by Mrs. Ruth Bohde, former minister to Denmark. The building of those dormitories, along with the other federally funded projects on campus, prompted a visit by Eleanor Roosevelt in September 1939. According to Ann Pearson, she delivered an address to an estimated five thousand people, remarking, "I am glad to see this remarkable institution and to observe the federal government's work on campus." It was an

extensive infusion of funds ($1.5 million) involving some thirteen major building projects.

During World War II, the trainees of the Army Specialized Training Program displaced the coeds in these living quarters. As in Auburn's early days, when male students wore cadet gray, men in uniform claimed the campus. The women reclaimed their rooms in April 1944.

During the early 1960s, the dormitories in both groups were named for outstanding women, while retaining their numerical designations: (I) Elizabeth Taylor Harper flanagan, (II) Katie Broun, (III) Willie Gertrude Little, (IV) Margaret Kate Teague, (V) Letitia Dowdell Ross, (VI) Maria Allen (Allie) Glenn, (VII) Mary Lane Petrie, (VIII) Ella Allemony Lupton, (IX) Helen Keller, (X) Marie Bankhead Owen, (XI) Annie White Mell, and (XII) Dana King Gatchell.

With the exception of Helen Keller and Marie Owen, these women were important figures in the early history of Auburn. Three of them, Katie Broun (daughter of President Broun), Willie Little, and Margaret Teague, represented the first women to graduate from Auburn. Each of the three was assisted to the podium during the ceremony by Governor Thomas Goode Jones "amid thunderous applause." The year was 1894.

The center of the upper quadrangle is one of the most successful of the outdoor rooms on campus. It is a Renaissance axial composition focused on Cater Hall [31] on the north and the Quad Center [33] on the south. With its magnificent live oaks, the space has the ambience one might expect in the groves of academe. It is a warm, sheltering space steeped in tradition.

The space may be endangered. The newest master plan for growth and development would eventually convert this area of the campus for more intensive academic use, while moving dormitories to the periphery. Let us hope that a concern for quality and a commitment to retaining open spaces will not be sacrificed for the sake of efficiency.

[33] THE QUAD CENTER 1939

Built as a dining hall to feed the residents of the Women's Quadrangle [32], it was expanded in 1952 as the dormitory complex was expanded. Food service at the Quad Center was discontinued sometime after the dining room for the Hill Dorms [62] and Foy Union's [12] cafeteria began operations.

After several years of relative idleness the building was completely renovated for office use. The Quad Center now houses the bursar's office as well as the editorial offices of *National Forum*, the international journal of Phi Kappa Phi Scholastic Honor Society.

[34] SPIDLE HALL 1962

Home economics instruction has been a part of Auburn's curriculum for a long time. The one-time Department of Foods and Clothing was shunted through a series of campus homes, before earning its own home base at Spidle Hall. The program achieved school status in 1929 and now claims about 560 student majors, besides providing service courses for many others.

Marion Walker Spidle, head professor and dean of home economics for twenty-eight years (1938–66), served the University as a distinguished member of the faculty for a total of forty-one years (1925–66). She held degrees from Montevallo and Columbia and was continually in leadership positions with the Alabama, American, and International Home Economics associations. In 1960, she was named Progressive Farmer's Woman of the Year in

Alabama. The Home Economics Alumni Association of Auburn has established a scholarship honoring Marion Spidle for her dedicated service.

In 1987, the University went through an organizational restructuring. In that process the School of Home Economics became the School of Human Sciences, a label that more precisely describes the directions of new programs that have evolved. Currently, three departments, consumer affairs, family and child development, and nutrition and foods, offer ten different curricula: clothing, textiles, fashion merchandising, family resource management, consumer economics, child development, interiors, housing, nutrition, and hotel and restaurant management.

[35] MELL HALL 1925

Although the records are hazy, apparently the Sigma Nus constructed this building as their campus residence in 1925, a time of unrestrained fraternity popularity. It must have been impressive with its pedimented portico and columns crowned with acanthus leaves.

There was a date room on the first floor—right next to the housemother's apartment. There were screened porches on both levels at each end. Upstairs, they were for open-air sleeping, following a national obsession with the health benefits to be derived therefrom. Downstairs, the porches were used for sitting or dining. These wings have now been

enclosed with board and batten siding to provide additional office space.

Mell Hall was incorporated into the Women's Quadrangle [32] as Dorm XI in the 1950s. Today, it serves as the central office for Auburn's continuing education programs.

[36] THE AVIARY 1974

One of the largest aviaries for a single occupant in the country, these generous living accommodations house War Eagle VI, mascot of all Auburn varsity teams. This famous golden eagle is nicknamed Tiger, which concentrates all the team pseudonyms in one eleven-pound nine-year-old bird. It is an awesome responsibility.

In addition to appearing at Auburn athletic events, Tiger makes hundreds of other appearances each year. To satisfy her public service commitments, she frequently accepts engagements at other schools to promote education about eagles. Who could be better qualified?

[37] HUMAN SCIENCES ANNEX 1956

Until recently, students in home economics education spent one quarter in residence here practicing the running of a household on a tight budget. Now, the building houses the University's extensive historic costume collection, which is used as a resource by students of fashion and textiles, and the new money management center.

[38] GLANTON HOUSE 1939

Originally a home management laboratory facility, this residential-style building was converted in 1973 to a marriage and family therapy center serving the School of Human Sciences. Louise Phillips Glanton was head professor of home economics from 1927 to 1937.

[39] CHILD STUDY CENTER 1939

With an enrollment of sixty two-and-a-half to five-year-olds, the Child Study Center is a friendly laboratory for research in behavior of pre-schoolers and a training site for family and child development majors.

[40] HALEY CENTER 1969

Built to relieve the pressure of an expanding enrollment in the late 1960s, Haley Center, Auburn's tower of learning, provided 384,000 square feet of additional academic space in one stroke. This building covers nearly two and a half acres and rises ten floors in height. It houses the University bookstore and serves most of the needs of the Colleges of Education and Liberal Arts. It can accommodate 8,500 students in classes at one time.

The first three floors, designed in quadrants connected by wide passageways, contain classrooms, teaching laboratories, and a 517-seat auditorium. These rooms are shared by all departments in Haley.

Rising from the center of the base is a ten-story tower containing offices, as well as seminar and conference rooms. There is a student lounge, a faculty lounge, and, on the south half of the third floor roof, a promenade deck.

Haley Center presents a clear, formal organization when viewed from the outside. The four equal quadrants define the entries and support the central tower. The geometry is irrefutable. Inside, however, the building's endless corridors have a sameness about them that can frustrate the uninitiated.

The paved-brick concourse walkway that links Haley with the rest of the campus has become an outdoor commons for student social and political interaction between classes. It is the pulse of the campus, a pulse that sometimes beats very loudly when reinforced with loudspeakers.

The top floor of Haley houses the Eagle's Nest, a student-faculty penthouse lounge that affords access to the roof and the best views of the entire campus.

The last stop on the elevator is floor nine, so the final leg to the Eagle's Nest must be negotiated by stairway. It is always open.

Paul Shields Haley served as an Auburn trustee for fifty-one years, and during that unparalleled period of service he missed only one meeting. He graduated in civil engineering in 1901 and distinguished himself in that profession. In 1961, Auburn awarded Dr. Haley an honorary Doctor of Science degree. In 1965, he was given the Algernon Sydney Sullivan Award "in recognition of such characteristics of heart, mind and conduct as evince a love for and helpfulness to others."

[41] PETRIE HALL 1939

Another legacy of the Public Works Administration, Petrie Hall was first a field house, though its classic Georgian demeanor makes it hard to imagine it in that role. It was also headquarters for the

athletic department until 1969, when Memorial Coliseum [80] opened its doors. A pair of openings in the limestone lobby walls, where ticket sales for athletic events once took place, serves as a reminder of Petrie Hall's former life.

Petrie Hall is now the home of the geology department. The lobby has become a mini-museum of rocks and fossils and includes pieces from a clidastes skeleton and the ever-popular mosasaurs, a family of extinct marine lizards. Some of the more interesting specimens are exclusively Alabamian and are clearly labeled.

George Petrie is another name that appears repeatedly in the history of Auburn's early days. According to *Lengthening Shadows*:

He was a dynamic history professor, 'a teacher without peers,' trainer of history teachers and scholars, [and] served Auburn as professor of modern languages, (1887–89), and Latin, and head professor of history (1891–1942). He was academic dean (1908–21), dean of graduate studies (1921–29), and graduate dean (1929–42). He started tennis at Auburn in 1888 and football in 1892. After retirement he wrote the 'Auburn Creed.'

The above account fails to mention that Dean Petrie not only brought football to Auburn, he also coached Auburn's first team, which defeated the University of Georgia in the Deep South's first major intercollegiate football game. The two teams met in Atlanta's Piedmont Park on February 22, 1892. The score was 10–0.

WALK TWO

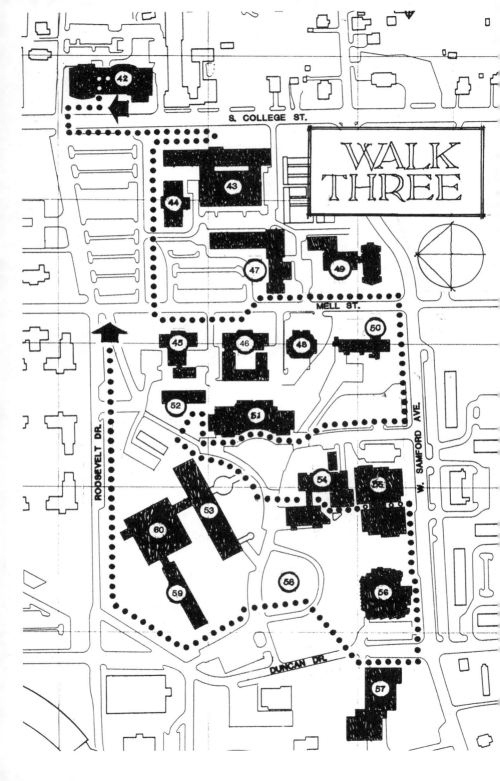

Walk Three
The South Campus

START THIS WALKING TOUR AT THE NEW ALUMNI Center on South College Street. After a visit to the lobby with its black granite wall honoring contributors, cross College Street at Roosevelt Drive, named for the thirty-second president of the United States, and you are in the Ag Hill area. This is a concentration of buildings serving the College of Agriculture, along with the Cooperative Extension Service and School of Forestry.

The science-mathematics complex and the fine arts buildings make up the balance of the group on this tour. These are the new kids on the block, and they are still growing. The Chemistry Building opened its doors for students for the fall quarter 1989, and a second chemistry building is being planned for the site just to the south of it. These new facilities meant the closing of Duggar Drive to through traffic and the loss of a large number of parking spaces for faculty and students. Auburn may eventually become a totally pedestrian campus as parking problems approach big-city proportions.

42	Alumni Center	51	Chemistry Building
43	Funchess Hall	52	Extension Annex
44	Comer Hall	53	Saunders Laboratory
45	Duncan Hall	54	Dudley Hall
46	Agricultural Engineering	55	Goodwin Hall
47	Animal Science	56	Telfair Peet Theatre
48	Animal Laboratory Building	57	Leach Nuclear Science Center
49	M. White Smith Hall	58	Graves Amphitheatre
50	Swingle Hall	59	Allison Hall
		60	Parker Hall

[42] ALUMNI CENTER 1989

The new Alumni Center puts the alumni association into a first-class, state-of-the-art facility to run the affairs of the very active alumni of Auburn

University. It replaces the outgrown quarters the association occupied in Foy Union [12].

Alumni now have an identifiable and prominent home when they are on campus—a place to meet friends, hold meetings and reunions, and renew their ties with their alma mater. The instructions to the architect, Joseph L. Donofro and Associates, were to

create a form that would be at peace with the old (for example, Comer Hall [44]) and in harmony with the new (for example, Harbert Center [26]). A black granite wall in the foyer is inscribed with the honor roll of contributors to the building fund. No taxpayer money went into the project.

Both the alumni and the development offices manage their many activities from here, such as the network of alumni clubs, the *Auburn Alumnews*, the alumni scholars and professorships, the placement service, the extension and research awards, and the business of keeping people happy with their football and basketball tickets. The annual giving program and other special fund raisers will be the continuous business of the center.

[43] Funchess Hall 1961

Modern laboratories and classrooms for research and teaching in the College of Agriculture became a reality with the completion of Funchess Hall. The science facilities allow chemical and biological experiments for research in soils, crop fertility, plant diseases, insect and weed control, and food processing. The updated laboratories also made possible the handling of radioisotopes and opened a new era of exacting research that has helped immensely in attracting and retaining highly competent faculty members.

Funchess Hall honors Marion Jacob Funchess for forty-one years (1909–50) of distinguished service as a teacher, researcher, and administrator. He fathered the agriculture experiment station system. Although an advocate of basic research, Dr. Funchess had a profound interest in its practical application to the farm, a reflection of his South Carolina farm heritage.

[44] COMER HALL 1909
(REBUILT 1922)

One of the more intriguing pieces of architecture on the campus, Comer Hall warrants close study. The building, classified as Second Renaissance Revival style, was designed by N. C.

Curtis, first head of the architecture department. It appears to have been conceived as a two-story classical composition with a third floor tacked on. It has a definite architecturally celebrated top above the ceiling line of the second floor with a wide continuous architrave, projecting cornice punctuated with dentils, and symmetrical gables capping the wings at each end. Above all this, almost as an afterthought sits another floor, faced in a different brick and with no real expression of top.

The designer may have wished to keep the proportions of a three-story building from being overwhelming. The building is scaled down through placement of bold detail at the top of the second floor and closer to the ground where the exuberant column capitals can be seen and appreciated. The change to a softer, lighter colored brick at the third story also helps minimize the building's height.

The architectural details, particularly the column capitals, are especially noteworthy. At the top of the tall columns, rams' heads are festooned with fruit and entwined with ears of ripe corn, grapes, and sheaves of wheat. The traditional acanthus leaves of a Corinthian column capital may, in this case, be cabbage.

Braxton Bragg Comer was one of Alabama's most progressive governors. He was very interested in Auburn's teaching, extension, and research programs in agriculture. The University enjoyed some unprecedented appropriations for buildings and instruction during his administration (1906–11). Apparently, The University of Alabama also benefited from his tour in office. That campus also has a Comer Hall.

[45] Duncan Hall 1928

Built as the state headquarters for the Alabama Cooperative Extension Service, Duncan Hall continues to fulfill this role to the present time. It is one of the few buildings of its age that has not had to adapt itself to traumatic change in purpose.

Duncan Hall is a contemporary of the Animal

Science [47] building across the street and bears a strong family resemblance. Warren, Knight and Davis were architects for both. Agricultural Engineering [46] and Extension Annex [52] were cut from the same cloth by the same architects ten years

later. The mirror glass windows in Duncan were not part of the original design. They were included in an extensive remodeling in recent years.

Luther Noble Duncan was Auburn's ninth president (1935–47) and longtime director of extension (1920–37). He came to the presidency from the triumvirate, or committee of three—John Wilmore in engineering, Bolling Crenshaw in mathematics, and Duncan in extension—that governed the University during the difficult years 1932 to 1935. These were the worst years of the depression.

The state failed to pay appropriations, salaries had to be reduced, and services were cut back dramatically. As if that were not enough, the Southern Association of Colleges and Secondary Schools placed Auburn on probation until full salaries could be paid and a higher level of student services resumed.

According to *Through the Years*, the situation was serious:

Faced as president with an indebtedness of over one million dollars in a continuing depression, a disgruntled faculty and staff, and growing pressure for physical expansion, Dr. Duncan rallied political support in the state and exploited every possible financial program of the New Deal. Before his death in 1947, the bonded indebtedness of the university was paid in full and 14 new buildings were added.

[46] AGRICULTURAL ENGINEERING 1939

Initially called the Farm Engineering Building, this was ne of thirteen projects of the ublic Works Administration program at Auburn. It is straightforward Georgian, as ᷉ most of the agriculture and tension group. A large anx was attached to the west side of the building in 1949.

[47] ANIMAL SCIENCE 1930, 1960

This L-shaped building was obviously built in two stages. The original portion has the authentic Georgian look so prevalent on campus. It is a symmetrical composition with strongly articulated center entry and balanced projecting wings at the ends, each

capped with a gable roof. Cut stone quoins, pilasters, keystones, sills, and a belt course provide a strong pattern in contrast with an Auburn red brick. A nicely proportioned classical arched window set behind an ornamental balustrade over the front entry gives the building an elegance that belies its utilitarian function.

The 1960 north-wing addition, on the other hand, suggests either a lower budget or a loss of conviction in the Georgian style as the appropriate expression for academic laboratories. It was designed during the period when all traditional styles were being discarded and may have been a compromise solution.

Initially, the building was called Animal and Dairy Science. It became Animal and Poultry Science after the creamery moved to Burke Laboratory. It is a teaching/laboratory facility dedicated to fundamental research to aid and promote all aspects of agribusiness. It reflects the considerable importance of everything agricultural in the development of Auburn University, Alabama's major land-grant institution.

[48] ANIMAL LABORATORY BUILDING 1988

This building serves a dual purpose. It expands the animal research capabilities of the University and houses a satellite steam generation plant to serve the neighborhood.

[49] M. WHITE SMITH HALL 1948, 1969

Forestry has been a major economic force in the state of Alabama since the mid-1800s and continues to be a vital factor to the present time. Auburn's School of Forestry, housed in M. White Smith Hall, supports this giant industry through continuous study and research.

The original building, designed by Sherlock, Smith and Adams, was Contemporary modified toward Classical Revival. The requisite symmetry and ornamented details are abandoned, but the classic two-story colonnaded portico is retained, albeit without embellishment.

The later addition matches the original in height and repeats the heavy, white continuous cornice.

Otherwise, it is a fresh treatment, reflecting changing architectural tastes over the twenty-year interval. Two devices, developed and widely distributed between the date of the initial building and its addition, can be observed: (1) the then-popular prefabricated curtain wall frames the windows that are blocked en masse and (2) tinted glass eases the intensity of southern sunlight.

M. White Smith was a prime organizer of the Alabama Forest Products Association and served as its second president. As a leader in the industry in the state, he took great interest in Auburn's educational and research programs in forestry. After his death in 1964, former associates campaigned to have the new forestry building named the M. White Smith Hall.

[50] SWINGLE HALL 1972

Auburn enjoys a worldwide reputation in the area of fisheries and aquaculture, the word coinage that suggests the potential for feeding a hungry world through farming the sea. Much of the credit for the leadership role in bringing this about goes to the man for whom this building is named. Homer Scott

Swingle arrived in Auburn in 1934 after completing graduate studies at Ohio State University. Almost immediately he started making significant discoveries in pond construction and management, fish population dynamics, and biological pest control. His experiments grew out of agricultural experiment station research projects directed originally toward the management of small freshwater ponds to assure farmers and sportsmen good fishing.

His research began attracting wide-ranging attention and support. Rockefeller Foundation money came in 1965. In 1970, Auburn was awarded a major grant by the Agency for International Development (AID) to strengthen competence in aquaculture and the International Center for Aquaculture was established at Auburn with Dr. Swingle as its head. In 1971, he was also made head of the new Department of fisheries and Allied Aquaculture.

The program continues to grow in reputation and stature. In 1988, another AID grant ($1.9 million) was given to Auburn to help Indonesia increase its production of fish, one of the island nation's main sources of protein. Over a three-year period a fisheries faculty member will live in Indonesia to coordinate the effort with three major Indonesian universities.

Swingle Hall is the headquarters for a large-scale fisheries operation, including acres of artificial ponds north of town. With ongoing expansion, these small lakes represent the world's finest facility for fish research, which could change the way the world eats.

[51] CHEMISTRY BUILDING 1989

This new laboratory building joins the other three buildings in the science-mathematics complex to relieve the pressure of expanded enrollment in the sciences. The architects, Barganier, McKee, Sims Associates, were challenged with a difficult site and with finding a way to relate the new facility to the existing three buildings, Saunders Laboratory [53], Allison Hall [59], and Parker Hall [60]. They chose to close Duggar Drive to vehicular traffic and to

WALK THREE

exercise the new freedom of the 1980s for strongly expressed three-dimensional volumes with suggestions of classic formality—a Post–modern building. To bridge the twenty-six years that separate the old and the new chemistry buildings, a pedestrian walkway was incorporated to physically tie them together.

[52] EXTENSION ANNEX 1938

Built ten years after Duncan Hall [45], this building reflects the growth in the extension program. Agricultural extension has been a major responsibility of Auburn from its land-grant beginnings, and continues, along with instruction and research, to be one of the primary missions of the University.

Known first as the AAA Building and later as Duncan Hall Extension Annex, the building houses the offices of extension specialists and the editorial offices. Across the drive is a white one-story building known as Extension Cottage.

[53] SAUNDERS LABORATORY 1963

The three buildings that form a science-mathematics triumvirate, Saunders Laboratory, Allison Hall [59], and Parker Hall [60], were designed by the same architectural team and constructed at one time. They bear a strong family resemblance, and the architectural impact of all three will be discussed here since they make a common statement.

Each building presents the stripped-down, no-frills, contemporary look of the 1960s, which is much maligned in the 1990s. The long, three-story blocks present flat, two-dimensional extruded facades, which are relieved only slightly by the rhythm of the vertical window treatment and by setbacks at the cornice and at the base. Further relief comes from the stand of tall pines and other trees that surround the building group and cast a pattern of shadows that soften their straight faces.

The whole assembly appears to be floating in a grassy moat. Access is by bridge at nearly all entries, and the buildings are joined to each other by glass-enclosed corridors or ramps.

The new Chemistry Building [51] in the same neighborhood brings relief to the over-crowding of the three science-mathematics facilities and is joined to Saunders by a pedestrian bridge. Cost estimates for renovating Saunders to meet future needs of the chemistry department appear to be prohibitive. Ironically, this means that Saunders will probably be converted to a new use and force the construction of a second chemistry building on the adjacent site to the south.

Charles Richard Saunders served Auburn's School of Chemistry from 1932 to 1968, the last eighteen years as dean. He retired in 1968, when chemistry became a part of the School of Arts and Sciences. Dr. Saunders completed his undergraduate work at Auburn, then went on to earn a doctorate at the University of Nebraska. After a tour as an instructor at Lafayette College, he worked as a research chemist for the DuPont Corporation before accepting the call to full-time academia.

[54] DUDLEY HALL 1977

Dudley Hall, housing both architecture and building science, is the third unit of what was originally planned as a fine arts complex. It was designed by Northington, Smith, and Kranert, who were also responsible for nearby Telfair Peet Theatre [56] and Goodwin Hall [55]. The long-range plan was to eventually construct facilities for all fine arts departments on this one block site.

With the organizational restructuring of the University in 1985, however, the Departments of music, art and theater were reassigned to the new College of Liberal Arts, and the dream of grouping the fine arts into one neat, identifiable location on campus makes

less theoretical sense than it once did.

Dudley Hall is the four-story L-shaped block that contains the studios, classrooms, computer laboratories, and offices serving the Departments of Architecture and Building Science. The two-story appendage linked to Dudley by a bridge houses the library, auditorium, gallery, snack bar, and the offices of the dean. This wing is called Fine Arts Commons. Working together, the two building masses form an outdoor living room. This space is articulated by a composition of solid rectangular brick blocks that serve as casual seating for between-class conversations or the many functions such as Honors Day and Fine Arts Week scheduled in this room.

A single red maple forms the focus of the space. It replaced a mature gum tree that failed to survive the trauma of the building's construction. The maple and its installation were the gift of the landscape architecture students, who were greatly distressed when it became clear that the old gum tree was dying a slow death. That was 1985. The new shade tree gets shadier every year.

Since Dudley is situated between the women's dormitories across Samford Avenue and the academic heart of the University, a way was provided for the dormitory residents to pass through the complex on their way to and from classes. The meandering path, moving across changing levels, under bridges, and past flowering plants, has the feeling of walking through a European hill town. The heavy traffic every hour as classes change makes this one of the liveliest spaces on campus.

The building honors Ralph Dudley, a 1918 Auburn graduate in civil engineering. He later completed a degree in architecture at Columbia. Mrs. Dudley directed that funds generated by the Dudley Foundation set up by her husband be used exclusively for the benefit of Auburn University and designated to the School of Architecture.

[55] GOODWIN HALL 1973

Built in three phases, as funds became available, Goodwin Hall is the home of the Department of Music. Phase I was the band building. The band actually moved to the new site in 1972, while the remainder of the department continued to operate in the old music building, now Hargis Hall [3]. Phase II included an orchestra rehearsal hall, as well as several teaching rooms and offices. Phase III was a two-story wing, which completed the facility.

The building is never quiet. The sounds of music emanate from practice and rehearsal rooms as the Auburn Knights, the marching band, the symphony orchestra, the choral group, the jazz band, the woodwind quintet, the brass ensemble, or individual students rehearse. It is active and alive, with an endless offering of quality musical events.

James Goodwin is a prominent consulting engineer and businessman in Birmingham. He graduated from Auburn in 1927 in civil engineering, not in music. But it was through a series of generous contributions from James and Virginia Goodwin that these facilities were made possible.

James Goodwin has performed many other services for Auburn over the years. He was a member of the Auburn University Foundation Board and a sponsor of the Generations Fund, which raised $111 million. The family has made gifts to support the library, professorships, the College of Veterinary Medicine, the new Alumni Center [42], and the endowment of the Philpott Eminent Scholar Chair in Religion.

The entry to Goodwin Hall and the fine arts complex boasts an unusual piece, the sculpture *Monody*. The eighteen-foot-high creation in bronze and brass by Jean Woodham is centered at the opening between the wings of the building. The artist's intent is

to "express and to communicate, through form, the feeling that music rises from the earth, soars to the heavens, and elevates the human spirit." Woodham, a graduate of Auburn's Department of Art and a former faculty member, recorded fifteen hundred hours of welding in the execution of this piece.

[56] TELFAIR PEET THEATRE 1973

Organized theatre activity began at Auburn in 1913. It was variously called dramatics, drama, and dramatic arts before being officially named the Department of Theatre in 1967. The department, whatever its name, made do in several campus venues, including Langdon Hall Annex [5] and the tower of Samford Hall [9], before settling in the 1930s into what is now the University Chapel [8]. The Y-Hut, as it was called then, seated 140 patrons, who faced a stage that was only nineteen feet wide and twelve feet high at the proscenium opening. These slight dimensions did not deter Professor Telfair Peet from attempting any play he and his students wished to undertake from twenty-five hundred years of Western dramatic literature. Professor Peet was an innovator who pioneered collegiate theatre at Auburn from 1931 until his sudden death in 1965 at age sixty-two.

After nearly fifty years in makeshift quarters, theatre activities in 1973 came to a proper focus in a state-of-the-art theatre building designed by

Northington, Smith, and Kranert in consultation with Dr. Cleveland Harrison, then head ʰeatre professor. The architect sought to make a statement that would contrast sharply with the pink red brick, white mortar, and trim that traditionally characterize Auburn buildings. To unify and suggest relationships, a dark red brick with matching mortar was selected along with bronze anodized windows and door frames for all the fine arts buildings. The theatre is the most exuberant and expressive of the three, almost acting out its role on campus. The Telfair Peet Theatre was formally dedicated on May 12, 1973.

The facility is one of the best arranged and best equipped college theatres in the South. The easily modified stage space, 36 feet wide at the proscenium opening and 110 feet in total width, has an elevator forestage and the potential for staging plays and musicals from any historical era. The bell-shaped auditorium, with continental seating for 405, is acoustically and visually outstanding. Generous spaces for scene and costume construction are contiguous to the stage. A handsome two-story lobby and mezzanine gallery greet the theatre visitor. The Telfair Peet Theatre was one of the first buildings on campus designed to accommodate the physically handicapped.

The old chapel, the theatre's former home, reputedly had a ghost, a British soldier of fortune who fought for the Confederacy in the Civil War and died in the chapel when it was being used as a hospital. Adding credence to the possibility of a ghost were the moans and creaks of the building's old timbers, as well as the eerie shadows cast by work lights late at night. Many theatre students have claimed to feel the palpable presence of Sidney, as he is called, especially after rehearsals when the cast was thinning out. When the theatre moved to its new building, Sidney reportedly came along with the scenery, costumes, and properties. He now roams in the dark recesses and halls of Telfair Peet Theatre, sometimes during rehearsals in the catwalks overhead, and always afterwards, when the steel superstructure snaps and creaks.

When it was dedicated, the Leach Nuclear Science Center enhanced the University's capacity for research and instruction in the fast-breaking twentieth-century realm of science. The facility, which contains twenty-eight laboratories on two floors, generates continuous studies in areas such as environmental impact and radiological safety.

In 1986, the addition of a twelve-thousand-square-foot clear span laboratory, which can be easily reconfigured to accommodate changing research needs, prepared the facility for twenty-first century expectations. The addition is Auburn's home for the extensively funded research associated with the Star Wars Initiative. The wing features high-load floors for heavy equipment, acoustically insulated floor pads, a photographic laboratory, and a machine shop. The building has compressed air, water, and 1.5 million watts of electric power (five or six times the normal capacity).

Edmund C. Leach was three times president of the Auburn Alumni Association and the first president of the Auburn University Foundation. At the dedication of this building President Draughon said, "I have known no man more loyal and devoted to his alma mater."

WALK THREE

The next notable stop on the tour is not a building at all; it is an outdoor room on the side of a hill, defined by a few well-placed stones set in the ground and surrounded by a stand of tall pines with a backdrop of red brick buidings. The amphitheatre is a magical place with a wonderful ambience that seems to touch everyone who visits it.

Construction of the graceful, undulating forms of the amphitheatre was accomplished with durable Belgian granite blocks donated by the city of Montgomery. The blocks were once the cobblestone surface of Commerce Street in downtown Montgomery. They came to the United States as ballast for empty sailing ships that were here to load cotton for European markets.

The site of the amphitheatre and the area around it were once covered by a series of small cottages. The first twenty-five of these, built in 1935 as a Public Works Administration project, were intended to house delegates who attended agricultural conferences. These were later converted to dormitories for Auburn athletes, until the completion of Sewell Hall [63] in 1962.

In September 1946, Auburn experienced a sudden heavy influx of discharged veterans, as did most colleges in the country. This demanded a rapid expansion of the faculty, which put a strain on available housing. Ffty-one family units, moved from Panama City, Florida, to serve as faculty apartments, created an instant village.

Some of these units survived into the early 1970s, making themselves useful as adjuncts to the Department of fisheries and Allied Aquacultures, until construction of Goodwin Hall [55] and Telfair Peet Theatre [56] forced their removal.

Graves Amphitheatre serves all constituencies of the campus for a variety of assemblies and performances throughout the year. It hosts everything from rock bands to symphony concerts, dramatic arts to dance, class lectures to pep rallies, and politics to picnics.

David Bibb Graves, an engineering graduate of
The University of Alabama and a Yale Law School
graduate, was Alabama's fortieth and forty-second
governor. His motto, which he passed on in a speech
to Auburn's 1935 graduating class, was "Keep On
Keeping On."

[59] ALLISON HALL 1963

The physics program and research efforts in the
physical sciences at Auburn owe much to Fred
Allison. For thirty-one years (1922–53), he shepherded the physics department as head professor
and concurrently served as graduate dean (1949–
53). He was an active researcher throughout his
life and achieved international recognition in the
field of magneto-optics. Dr. Allison shares with his

colleagues the discovery of chemical elements 85 and 87 and a heavy isotope of hydrogen.

He remained on the faculty at Auburn until he was seventy. He then accepted teaching assign-

ments at two other colleges and continued his private research. Dr. Allison died in 1974 at the age of ninety-two.

The architectural treatment of Allison Hall is a photocopy of Saunders Laboratory [53] and similar to that of Parker Hall [60]. The straight forward handling of the block without embellishment may be entirely appropriate for the discipline involved. It is discussed in some detail under the description of Saunders Laboratory.

[60] PARKER HALL 1963

William Vann Parker was named head of mathematics at Auburn in 1950 and dean of the Graduate School in 1953. Holding degrees from North Carolina, Princeton, and Brown, he had taught at Sewanee, North Carolina, Princeton, and Mississippi State College for Women before coming to Auburn. Dean Parker made many contributions to the literature of mathematics and co-authored the book *Matrices*.

Architecturally, Parker Hall is much like the other two in the science-mathematics complex, except that the windows are stacked in pairs rather than being single. Parker acts as a symbolic center to the complex. A glass-box entry is appended to the long flat facade, offering some form relief.

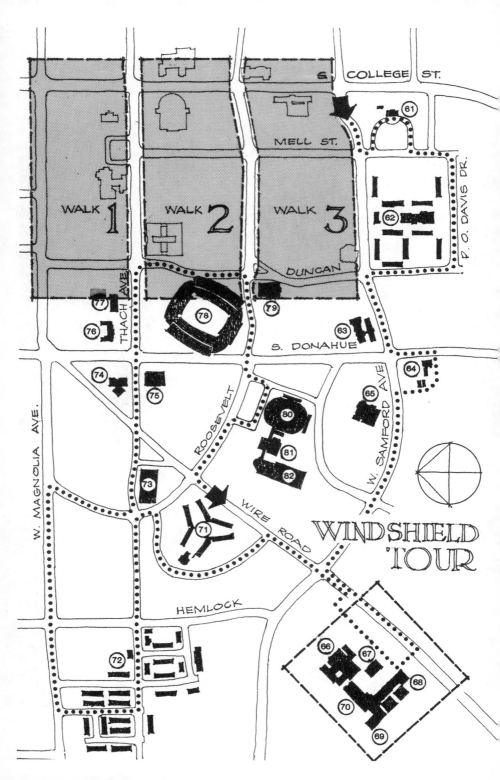

Tour Four
The Windshield Tour
(THE EXTENDED CAMPUS)

O THER BUILDINGS ON THE CAMPUS ARE too scattered to visit comfortably on foot, so this last tour is intended to be negotiated by car.

Start your tour at the President's Home on Mell Street. Most of the buildings on this tour are among the more recent additions, which accounts in part for their location on the periphery rather than in the central campus area. They include the primary residential buildings, sports facilities, and the College of Veterinary Medicine. The veterinarians moved to their country campus, beginning in 1960, to gain space for animals to move and graze as the central area became increasingly crowded and more populated.

All facilities are open to the public. The lobby areas of the Athletic Center and the Nichols Center may warrant stops. The Honor Room in the Athletic Center displays the mementos of a thousand victories—and a few defeats—and may be of special interest to sports-minded visitors.

61 The President's Home
62 The Hill Dorms
   (Women's Dormitories)
63 Sewell Hall
64 Telecommunications
   and Educational TV
65 The Athletic Center
66 Greene Hall
67 Overton-Rudd
68 McAdory Hall
69 Scott-Ritchey
   Laboratories
70 Hoerlein Hall
71 Caroline Draughon
   Village Extension
72 Caroline Draughon
   Village

73 The Hangar
74 Nichols Center
75 George C. Wallace
   Center
76 Cary Hall
77 Miller Hall
78 Jordan-Hare
   Stadium
79 Sports Arena
80 Eaves-Memorial
   Coliseum
81 Swimming Pool /
   Auxiliary
   Gymnasium
82 The Student Ac-
   tivities Center

[61] The President's Home 1939

Appropriately Southern and Colonial Revival in style, the building has the proper look for a president's mansion: pristine white, with six stately wooden columns supporting the porch roof that extends across the entire front of the two-story central block. There are five gabled dormers behind a balustrade, and chimneys at each end are flanked with quarter-round lights. The house, which contains

6,750 square feet, was built for $38,412 in 1939. Imagine what it would cost today.

This imposing residence was the first of the Public Works Administration projects awarded to the campus in the late 1930s.

Other buildings contracted with the infusion of federal funds were Dorms I through IV at the Women's Quadrangle [32], Drake Student Health Center [21], the Practice House (now Glanton House [38]), Nursery School (now Child Study Center [39]), Farm Engineering Building (now Agricultural

Engineering [46]), the first portion of Jordan-Hare Stadium [78] west stands, and Tichenor [13], Petrie [41], and Cary [76] halls. All of these projects were started between November 1938 and November 1939. It was a heady time for Auburn: the beginning of the end of the long drought of the Great Depression.

This extensive federal involvement may have inspired the visit to the campus by the personable President Franklin Delano Roosevelt on March 30, 1939. He rode through the campus in a motorcade and was welcomed by President L. N. Duncan. He delivered a speech behind the quad dorms, which started with the well-known words, "My friends." It was the first time a U.S. President had visited Auburn, and the *Lee County Bulletin* said it looked like all of East Alabama was present. An appreciative University honored the president by naming a campus street Roosevelt Drive.

The President's home is, of course, also the domain of the first lady of Auburn. Each of the five mistresses who have occupied the residence has added her own touches, and many of the changes in decor and furnishings have stayed on past her residency.

The first occupants, the Duncans, furnished the house with pieces from the former presidential residence, including a Duncan Phyfe breakfast table with matching sideboard and chest. The Draughons added casual rattan furniture in the sunroom and a silver tea service with a tea cart. The Philpott legacy included a generously proportioned antique Federal dining room table with a set of Chippendale dining chairs. Two handsome needlepoint seats for the chairs in the entry hall were donated during that era. The Funderburks took on responsibility for a rather complete renovation: new carpeting, draperies, wallpaper, and paint colors. They also had the kitchen and butler's pantry updated with new cabinet work and appliances.

President and Mrs. Jim Martin are adding their own touches to personalize the presidential environment. The sunroom now contains a spinet piano that President Martin, a self-taught musician, enjoys in spare moments. Over the fireplace, Mrs. Martin has placed a quilted wall hanging, a gift from the board of trustees at the University of Arkansas, the Martins' last assignment before coming to Auburn.

Certain items predate the house itself. A small antique desk, twin beds, a dresser, and chest from the Thach era were moved from the old president's home, now the Social Center [31]. Other items were gifts. A grandfather clock, a secretary, and a collection of books came from the estate of Governor Henderson. The oversized mahogany clock was delivered to Auburn in a hearse, so the story goes. Actually, it was a vehicle that served the infirmary as ambulance. The handsome antique English secretary bears a plaque inscribed Laura Montgomery Henderson Memorial Room.

The interior of the President's Home is an amalgamation of many tastes and times, respectfully assembled over many years and saturated with Auburn history. It can only grow richer with time.

[62] THE HILL DORMS (WOMEN'S DORMITORIES) 1962–1967

Housing all female students in University-owned-and-operated dormitories was the rule at Auburn until 1976 when the numbers overwhelmed the capacity and pressure mounted for equal treatment under new federal laws. The first three new dorms (A, B, and C) were completed in 1962. To the great pride and comfort of the occupants, they were the first

housing units on campus to be air-conditioned. Terrell dining hall (Building I) was also opened in 1962 and expanded later to accommodate the total population of the Hill Dorms. Dorms D, E, and F followed in 1965 and G, H, J, and K in 1967. Building L, the administration building, was also completed in 1967.

All sororities on campus are accommodated in University housing. (By agreement of their national organizations they are not permitted to own their own houses.) Which sorority would be given first choice of location became a hot topic, according to Ann Pearson, one of the first occupants of the Hill Dorms. "It was finally decided it would be done on the basis of date of founding on the campus." That honor went to the Kappa Deltas, who chose Dorm B, perhaps because it was closest to the dining hall.

The Hill Dorms are now being completely renovated on a staggered schedule. The original design was rather austere, typical 1960s bare-bones institutional, flat-roofed architecture. The change is total. It includes an entirely new brick facing in two tones, warm red and deep brown, hip roofs with simulated dormers, and a stronger celebration of the central entry. The boxiness is alleviated by incorporating a series of brick piers and walls that conceal a ramp for handicapped students.

As in the Women's Quadrangle [32] dormitories, each of the twelve buildings is named to honor a woman who played a significant role in the history of the University or the community: (A) Mollie Hollifield Jones, (B) Annie Smith Duncan, (C) Marguerite Toomer, (D) Zoe Dobbs, (E) Berta Dunn, (F) Dixie Bibb Graves, (G) Camille Early Dowell, (H) Stella W. Knapp, (I) Leila Avary Terrell, (J) May Wright Boyd, (K) Sarah Hall Sasnett, and (L) Mattie Lucille Burton. Four of the women were wives of past Auburn presidents.

The dining hall is appropriately named for Leila Terrell, who operated a boarding house for students and professors for many years. On her ninety-fifth birthday, the board of trustees passed a resolution recognizing the great inspiration she had been to hundreds of students to whom she had given motherly care and counsel. She died in 1970 at age 104.

The Hill Dorms serve as home to more than 1,300 women each year. The complex is soon to be expanded, with three new buildings projected to house an additional 600 students, one-third of whom will be men.

[63] SEWELL HALL 1962, 1984

Sewell Hall is home to Auburn's varsity football and basketball athletes. The dormitory has seventy-two rooms, for 144 men, and a dining hall that serves gargantuan meals three times a day. An annex at the rear provides a study hall, a hospitality room, a game room, and three apartments for coaches.

What you see is a new Sewell Hall. The dormitory portion was gutted and completely remodeled in 1984, giving it a contemporary, first-class resort appearance.

Roy Brown Sewell, class of '22, came to be

known as Mr. Auburn. He was a truly dedicated and perpetually enthusiastic supporter of everything Auburn. While building a successful clothing manufacturing business in Breman, Georgia, he found time to serve as a founding member of the board of the Auburn Foundation, president of the National Alumni Association, president of the Atlanta Auburn Club, chairman of the Engineering Emergency Fund Drive, and honorary chairman of the fund drive for the new Alummi Center [42]. However, as the *Auburn Alumnews* pointed out in its August-September 1988 issue, most alumni will remember him first as the man who commissioned a New York song-writing team to write a fight song that would rival Georgia Tech's. The result was "War Eagle."

The *Alumnews* also praised Roy Sewell's positive attitude and sense of humor, which may have helped sustain him growing up in rural Randolph County as one of eleven children. Sewell himself loved to tell about his coming to Auburn in 1918, unsure of what to study, but determined to get away from the farm. A faculty member suggested pharmacy. Sewell quickly replied, "No, no, not pharmacy. I came to Auburn to get away from the pharm."

Because of his many services and deep devotion to Auburn, an honorary Doctor of Laws degree was conferred on Roy Sewell in 1958. He died on June 17, 1988, after a short illness. He was ninety.

[64] Telecommunications and Educational TV 1955

This is not, as many assume, a transmitting television station, but a service division whose primary mission is management of the University's telecommunications system. The professional staff also provides technical assistance for media projects and produce television documentaries and public service announcements for the Alabama Public Television network's regional and national distribution.

TOUR FOUR

[65] THE ATHLETIC CENTER 1989

While it was built primarily for Auburn football Tigers, the new facility helped relieve the crowded condition of Eaves-Memorial Coliseum [80]. Prior to construction of the Center, all varsity sports and physical education programs were housed under one roof. Now, the offices formerly occupied by football personnel accommodate basketball staff members and non-revenue sports and physical education people. According to the sports information office, "The new building, known for now as the Athletic Center, provides everything needed to insure that the young men representing Auburn will have the opportunity to be as good as they can be both on the football field and in the classroom."

The building houses team meeting rooms, state-of-the-art training and rehabilitation areas, world-class weight lifting rooms, special television equipment, and a film editing room. It includes offices for the athletic director, associate director, football coaches, business manager, academic counselor, and sports information.

Another feature of the Center is the Hall of Honor, which documents Auburn's athletic heritage. A display of loving cups, medals, photographs, and ribbons tell the stories of athletic contests through the years. These mementos trigger the memories of glorious moments and add color to a rich tradition.

Looming in the background of the Athletic Center like a cumulus cloud descended to earth is the football practice shelter. The six tons of polyester and cable are kept upright by two electric blowers with automatic backup generators. A revolving door provides access for players, and there is an airlock entry for vehicles. Practice sessions need never be rained out.

[66] GREENE HALL 1971

Initially called the Basic Sciences Building, this facility provides 120,000 square feet for classrooms and four general areas of study: anatomy and histology, physiology and pharmacology, pathology and parasitology, and microbiology. The administrative offices of the College of Veterinary Medicine are also here. Out front, in the architectural massing is the veterinary library, expressing the importance of this collection of shared knowledge.

Greene Hall was dedicated in a common ceremony with the Small Animal Clinic, now Hoerlein Hall [70] on November 7, 1971. President Harry Philpott remarked that the School of Veterinary Medicine had finally "got it all together," referring to the move from the central campus to the 240-acre Wire Road site, when Greene Hall and the Small Animal Clinic joined the first two veterinary facilities to be completed. McAdory Hall [68] and the Sugg Animal Health Laboratory (not included on tour) date from 1961.

Dedication ceremonies to change the name of the Basic Sciences Building to the James E. Greene Hall were held in November 1978. Dr. Greene contributed forty years of dedicated service to Auburn. He was a pioneer in establishing small animal medicine as a distinct discipline, and in 1948 he became head of Auburn's Department of Small Animal Surgery and Medicine. In 1958, following the death of Dean Redding S. Sugg, Greene was appointed dean of the school, only the fourth person to serve in that capacity.

At the time of the renaming, the *AU Report* noted that

under his administration the school experienced unparalleled growth with the student body increasing by 45 percent and the faculty and staff growing fourfold. Dean Greene was a national leader in the early efforts of the American Veterinary Medical Association to standardize quality professional education. For these efforts and others, he was elected by the AVMA in 1975 to receive the association's highest honor, the AVMA Award.

He died of a sudden heart attack in 1977, just twenty days after he retired.

[67] JOHN W. OVERTON AUDITORIUM–JOY GOODWIN RUDD STUDENT CENTER 1987

This bold contemporary building is the latest addition to the veterinary medicine complex and brings needed amenities to round out the facilities of the College's somewhat isolated campus. Overton Auditorium accommodates more than four hundred people in comfortable theatre-type seats and boasts the latest audiovisual equipment. It gives the College of Veterinary Medicine the capability of hosting conferences and seminars for veterinarians and provides the space for large gatherings of students and faculty.

Complementing the auditorium are the facilities of the Rudd Student Center: a student lounge, study rooms, computer areas, conference rooms, and an

informal dining space. Until the center became a reality, veterinary students had no place to relax,
snack, or study between classes because of the dis-
tance to the main campus.

The late John W. Overton was an active businessman in Montgomery, prominent in civic affairs, in-
fluential in political activities, and well known to
many mayors, governors, and even presidents. A
1935 graduate of Auburn, he was a dedicated supporter of the University, as evidenced by his service
on the board of trustees from 1959 to 1971.

The Joy Goodwin Rudd Student Center is named
in honor of a 1975 Auburn graduate, the daughter of
James and Virginia Goodwin. This building, along
with Goodwin Hall [55], was made possible through
the generosity of the Goodwins.

[68] McAdory Hall 1961

With the erection of McAdory Hall, the decision
was made to move the College of Veterinary Medicine to open land away from the increasingly
crowded main campus. It was the first of many
buildings to be constructed on the site. The facilities
of Auburn's Department of Large Animal Surgery

and Medicine are housed here: the main building, nine hospital barns, two research barns, a storage barn, ten large paddocks, 125 acres of pasture, and a five-eighths mile exercise track. There is a complete separation of the business activities and the care of patients from teaching areas. The hospital provides facilities for a patient population consisting of beef and dairy cattle, horses, sheep, swine, and occasionally, wild and exotic species.

Isaac Sadler McAdory was the second dean of the college. A 1904 Auburn graduate, he received his Doctor of Veterinary Medicine degree from McKillips Veterinary College in Chicago in 1908 and returned to Auburn that same year to join the veterinary staff. Dr. McAdory compiled an impressive forty-eight years of continuous service as a teacher, serving concurrently as acting dean (1935–37), dean (1937–40), state veterinarian (1935–40), and associate state veterinarian (1940–52). A fine professor and a favorite of students, Dr. McAdory resigned as dean in 1940 to give full attention to his first love, teaching.

During Dean C. A. Cary's lifetime (see Cary Hall [76]), Dr. McAdory was his faithful assistant and second in command. Dean Cary had recruited him while Isaac McAdory was still an Auburn undergraduate. When he returned to Auburn from Chicago, Dr. McAdory became Dean Cary's respected colleague and heir apparent. When Dean Cary broke his leg in a fall from the roof of his home, he would not let the local physicians touch it. Instead, Dean

Cary insisted that Dr. McAdory set the leg and administer to the recovery, which he did.

One of the more prominent patients to be treated at McAdory Hall was Bold Ruler, the nation's top race horse in 1957. His achievement on the track, however, was overshadowed by his success as a sire. In the first seven years after his retirement from racing, he sired an astonishing number of sons and daughters—eighty-two in all—many of whom won high stakes races. Eleven of them were named national champions.

Bold Ruler was admitted to medical care at Auburn in 1971 suffering from a malignant nasal tumor. The treatment included cobalt therapy, which meant transporting the oversized patient to the Leach Nuclear Science Center [57]. The thoroughbred survived for one year after his Auburn treatment. Bold Ruler's son Secretariat was a foal at the time. He went on to win the Triple Crown in 1973 and sire the 1986 Horse of the Year, Lady Secret.

[69] SCOTT-RITCHEY LABORATORIES 1979, 1984

This modern research laboratory branches westward from the junction of McAdory [68] and Hoerlein [70] halls. It was financed in its entirety through the generosity of contributors, of whom the two major ones were K. A. Scott and Eleanor Ritchey.

Mr. Scott was an avid sportsman and lifelong dog fancier from Cleveland, Ohio, who also had a home in Ethelsville, Alabama. He was surprised to learn there was virtually no research being done in the study of disorders and diseases of small pets. In 1955, through his generosity and that of other individuals, breed and kennel clubs, and veterinary associations, pioneer investigations were launched at Auburn in cardiology and neurology.

Eleanor Ritchey of Fort Lauderdale was an oil heiress who had a fondness for small animals. At the time of her death in 1968, she was caring for some

150 stray dogs, for whom she had great affection. Miss Ritchey left an estate of $4.2 million to Auburn's School of Veterinary Medicine, with the provision that these dogs be cared for during the remainder of their lives or for twenty years—whichever came first. The balance of the estate at that time was to support research on the spontaneous diseases of small pets that had been initiated by the Scott bequest. By the time the last dog, Musketeer, died on June 4, 1984, the estate had grown with interest to $12 million.

Phase I of the research facility was completed in 1979 and phase II in 1984. The Scott-Ritchey Laboratories represent one of the most modern and efficient multipurpose research facilities in the world. The core personnel supported by the program include seven faculty members, seven staff members, one postdoctoral fellow, a research associate, eight graduate students, eight technicians, and seven student assistants.

The name is new, but the building has been a functioning part of the veterinary medicine program since 1970. It was known as the Small Animal Clinic until November 13, 1988, when it was renamed Hoerlein Hall to honor a distinguished member of the faculty who retired in June 1984, after thirty-seven years of exceptional accomplishment.

Benjamin Franklin Hoerlein was head of Small Animal Surgery and Medicine for over twenty years at Auburn, during which time he established an international reputation for his contributions in clinical neurology, neurosurgery, and veterinary education. When the generous bequests from K. A. Scott and Eleanor Ritchey made possible the greatly expanded research into diseases of small animals, Dr. Hoerlein was named director of that research program.

In 1985, the American College of Veterinary Surgeons established a new mechanism to recognize those persons who have achieved unusual eminence in veterinary surgery. They called it the Distinguished Service Award, and Dr. Hoerlein was its first recipient.

Hoerlein Hall is not a separate and distinct entity but one of three wings of a larger building complex. McAdory Hall [68] and the Scott-Ritchey Laboratories [69] form the other two. Each wing was constructed at a different time for a specific purpose and bears a different title. A heavy over-structured canopy distinguishes Hoerlein from the others and provides a protective shelter for clients bringing their pets to the clinic—or is it the small animals who are the clients?

[71] CAROLINE DRAUGHON VILLAGE EXTENSION 1979

Built twenty years after the first Draughon Village Apartments [72], these six building blocks, three stories in height, accommodate 552 students in 138 apartments. The make-up is about half male and half female. A multipurpose lounge-study area takes the place of a living room in each apartment. The concept presents an alternative living arrangement to traditional dormitory life in an atmosphere that is close to residential in feeling.

[72] CAROLINE DRAUGHON VILLAGE 1959

The first group of two-story apartments built contiguous to the campus, these residences consist of 384 units. They are occupied primarily by married or graduate students and provide accommodations close to campus at moderate cost.

The buildings were sited to preserve a number of healthy trees and to flow with the natural contours of the land. A verdant valley replete with kudzu is kept intact, and each unit fronts on a grassy buffer strip. The Village has indeed become a village, and occupants, albeit temporary, report feeling part of a community.

Caroline Marshall Draughon, wife of Ralph Draughon, Auburn's tenth president, was involved in every happening that affected the well-being of the

college. Dr. Draughon often called her the Chancellor of Auburn University. The couple had a genuine warmth that endeared them to everyone.

Caroline Draughon was a graduate of Huntingdon College and in 1963 she received the Achievement Award, the highest honor conferred by that school's Alumni Association. The award cited her influence on the thousands of young men and women who had passed through Auburn during her tenure as its president's wife.

[73] THE HANGAR 1948

Two airplane hangars designed for use in World War II were joined together to enclose an enormous space (140 x 320 feet) for use in the ROTC programs. The hangar, which is on the site of a one-time golf course, is still used for pistol and rifle marksmanship, wilderness training, and special ranger classes.

[74] NICHOLS CENTER 1986

A recent addition to the campus, the Nichols Center is the home of the three ROTC programs: Navy, Army, and Air Force. Auburn has a long tradition, dating from the Civil War, of providing a training ground for military officers. The programs remain popular today, though they are no longer compulsory.

The four-column portico, which forms the impressive center piece of this symmetrical architectural composition, was transplanted from a former Auburn landmark, the "late" Broun Hall. Old Broun hall was a prominent presence on Magnolia Avenue, just off North College, from 1906 until it became a victim of progress in 1984. It was razed to make room for the newest engineering laboratory building, Harbert Center [26]. Many faculty members, students, and townspeople felt a key piece of the Auburn heritage was being lost forever. The compromise was the salvage of one of old Broun Hall's most prominent features, this massive stone portico, and its relocation to the new ROTC building.

Inside the lobby of the center stands *Bold Spirit*, a thirteen-foot sculpture designed by Professor Louis Abney and donated by the building architects, Barganier, McKee, Sims and Associates. The sculpture of laminated red oak, white oak, maple, and stainless steel can be seen as an eagle, a symbol of the military, as well as Auburn's mascot.

The building honors William F. Nichols, an Auburn graduate, U.S. congressman, and a member of Auburn's board of trustees for twenty years. His sudden death in the fall of 1988 was a great shock to the people of Alabama.

[75] GEORGE C. WALLACE CENTER FOR VOCATIONAL AND ADULT EDUCATION 1984

The Center for Vocational and Adult Education is a broadly based University program for preparing professional personnel, conducting research and program development activities, and providing services to education agencies, business, and industries.

The honoree's name has been a household word in Alabama for many years, and he may well be the best-known Alabamian in the nation. George

Wallace was a feisty and frequent governor, serving a total of four terms. His first wife, Lurleen, was also governor for part of a term until her death in 1968.

Governor Wallace took his message to the rest of the nation in the presidential campaigns of 1968 and 1972. He gained surprising support in such far-flung states as Michigan and Maryland. It was in Laurel, Maryland, on May 15, 1972, that four bullets dramatically changed his life and left him confined to a wheel-chair. George Corley Wallace retired from political life in 1987.

[76] CARY HALL 1940

The life of Charles Allen Cary is the saga of a remarkable man. He was, by all accounts, responsible for bringing an enlightened program of meat and food inspection to Alabama, establishing professionalism in the practice of veterinary medicine in the state, and directing the growth and development of Auburn's College of Veterinary Medicine.

Dr. Cary graduated from Iowa State College in 1887. After several years of practice, teaching, and further study in Germany, he happened to meet President William Broun of Auburn on a train. Dr. Broun persuaded Dr. Cary to come to Auburn to teach physiology and veterinary science. He arrived on the tiny campus in 1892, and one of his primary concerns became public health. In 1893, he began work as the experiment station veterinarian. His assignment was to attack the problems that Alabama farmers were having with their swine, poultry, and beef cattle production, thereby helping to provide a safe supply of milk and meat to consumers.

In 1907, Dr. Cary was named both the first dean of the newly created College of Veterinary Medicine and state veterinarian. His campaign to rid the state of ticks, tick fever, bovine tuberculosis, and brucellosis was highly successful and made the phenomenal growth of Alabama's beef cattle industry possible. He died in 1935 while still very much involved in the affairs of the college and the good health of the state of Alabama.

Cary Hall is cut out of the same architectural fabric as many of its peers on campus—a Georgian building with a projected central entry, capped with a gable and decorated with stone corner quoins. It stands as a poignant reminder of Vet Hill, which was home to many generations of veterinary students. Today, it is used primarily for the teaching of biology.

[77] MILLER HALL 1952

Designed by Shaw and Renneker, Miller Hall resisted major changes taking place in architectural expression following World War II and instead duplicated the predominant Georgian style on campus. It was originally devoted exclusively to the teaching of pharmacy, but now is home to Auburn's newest professional program, nursing.

The School of Nursing was conceived and implemented in record time. Funds were first appropriated in 1978. A dean, two faculty members, and an academic adviser put together a curriculum, policies, and procedures in the spring of 1979, and the first students were admitted that fall. The class numbered twenty-seven, twenty-four of whom went on to receive their bachelor's degrees in 1981.

Emerson R. Miller is identified with the beginning of pharmacy education in Alabama. He came to Auburn as the first teacher of pharmacy in 1895, after exceptional training at the Universities of Michigan, Marburg (Germany), and Minnesota. He was named professor of pharmacy a year later, and

except for time spent at experiment stations in
Santiago, Las Vegas, Cuba, and the University of
Wisconsin, he remained at Auburn, serving with
great dedication until his death in 1929. Professor
Miller had accumulated an extensive private library,
which was divided between chemistry and pharmacy.

[78] JORDAN-HARE STADIUM 1939

The stadium, that enormous structure looming over
the central campus, wasn't always such a command-
ing presence on campus. It has grown as Auburn's
reputation as a football power has grown.

The Tigers opened the Auburn Stadium in 1939
with a capacity crowd of 7,440 in a Southeastern
Conference game with Florida that ended in a 7–7
tie. It was renamed Cliff Hare Stadium in 1949 when
14,000 seats were added on the east sidelines. The
coaching success of Ralph ("Shug") Jordan in the
early 1950s created the need for additional seats.
Fourteen thousand were added in 1956, and in 1970
end zone stands were erected, completing a bowl
with a capacity of 61,261. The stadium was enlarged
again in 1980 to seat 72,109. With the completion
of the eastside upper deck for the 1987 season, the

capacity now stands at over 85,000 spectators. This makes Jordan-Hare the fifth largest on-campus stadium in the nation.

Cliff Hare was a member of Auburn's first football team in 1892. He later became dean of the School of Chemistry and was state chemist from 1930 to 1948. He taught physical and organic chemistry at Auburn for fifty years and headed the faculty athletic committee for much of that period. The Cliff

Hare Award, established in his memory, is given annually to the outstanding senior athlete.

Ralph ("Shug") Jordan was also a member of the Auburn football squad, as well as the basketball and baseball teams of the early 1930s. Hitting a homerun and pitching in the baseball championship victory over Florida and leading the basketball team to the semifinals were among the highlights of his career as an athlete. The Auburn Tigers were suffering lean years on the gridiron when Shug was brought back to the campus as head coach in 1951. He stayed in that job for twenty-five years, compiling twenty-one winning seasons (175 wins, 83 losses, 7 ties). His team went twenty-four games without a loss in 1956–58 and was named national champion by the Associated Press in 1957.

The latest addition, the eastside upper deck, completes the symmetry of the ring and the dominance of this monolith. The very size of the stadium symbolizes the tremendous attachment Auburn fans have for their game and their team. This concrete colossus occupies a prominent position near the center of everything on the campus.

[79] Sports Arena 1948

A war surplus building, the Sports Arena was dismantled at Camp Livingston, Louisiana, and re-erected on this site through the efforts of President Duncan and Senator Lister Hill. It was home to the

varsity basketball team until completion of the Coliseum [80] in 1969. Now it serves the University's
gymnastics team and gymnastics classes.

[80] EAVES-MEMORIAL COLISEUM 1969

The Coliseum was a longtime dream at Auburn.
The hoping and planning began in earnest with the
appointment of the first auditorium-arena committee
twenty-two years before the huge complex became
a reality.

The structure is a heavily programmed facility,
hosting a multitude of sporting events, concerts, lectures, clinics, and physical education classes. There
are thirteen thousand seats for major athletic events,
and the space can be subdivided for smaller audi-
ences by the placement of an enormous curtain.

Honeycombed around and under the tiered seating are the auxiliary support spaces: the main lobby,
ticket booths, public restrooms, concession stands,
and equipment for television coverage of events. Offices for the athletic coaches, public information
staff, and the facility manager, as well as classrooms
and offices for the Department of Health and Human Performance, are on the second level. The first
floor houses locker rooms, weight training facilities,
laundry and equipment rooms, and the Coliseum
machinery.

Originally dedicated to the memory of some 250
Auburn alumni who died in the four U.S. wars of this
century, the Coliseum was rechristened on February
10, 1988, when an additional name was added to the
250 previous honorees. Joel H. Eaves, a 1937 Auburn graduate and a star athlete in football, basketball, and baseball, returned to his alma mater as basketball coach in 1949, after a successful record as a
high school coach in Atlanta. In the next fourteen
years, he compiled a 214–99 record, and his team
won the regular-season Southeastern Conference basketball championship in 1960, Auburn's first. The renaming ceremony was held, appropriately, at half-
time of a regular-season game with Kentucky.

For years, President Philpott never failed to close
his remarks at June and August commencement exercises, when temperatures in the big room could top
ninety-five degrees, with the suggestion that anyone
wishing to make a meaningful contribution to the
University might do so by providing the means to
air-condition the Coliseum. This finally came to pass
in 1986 in time for the June commencement ceremony—to the great relief of everyone in attendance.

[81] SWIMMING POOL/AUXILIARY GYMNASIUM 1969

Linking the Coliseum [80] and the Student Activities Center [82] is a combination gymnasium and
swimming pool facility that serves the varsity swim
team and recreational programs. Current planning
includes the addition of a pool of Olympic proportions. At an approved budget of $6 million it should
be a world-class facility.

TOUR FOUR

The history of the Student Activities Center actually goes back to 1976 when students, led by Student Government Association President Buck Ruffin, voiced a need for the facility. In 1979, the question was put on a ballot and the student body voted to assess themselves an additional $8.50 in quarterly activity fees to finance construction of the project. High interest rates delayed progress for another three years, but finally plans were drawn by Pearson, Humphries and Jones and bids were received on the $6-million structure.

Designed with two levels, the center contains seven basketball courts, three of which are in a multipurpose arena adaptable for seating from six hundred to two thousand spectators. Other features include a game room, weight room, an all-purpose room, a snack bar, administrative offices, and the Greg Pratt Room. Greg Pratt was a varsity fullback who died during football practice on a very hot day preceding the 1983 season. This room honors him and the spirit and dedication he brought to Auburn.

Building Index